HIGHER

RMPS
RELIGIOUS & PHILOSOPHICAL QUESTIONS

SECOND EDITION

Joe Walker

Acknowledgements

The author would like to thank Lorna and David once more for all their support, encouragement and understanding since I first began this writing thing 27 years ago.

Thanks to all of you out there delivering and supporting RMPS. Keep up the good work.

The publishers would like to thank the following individuals, institutions and companies for permission to reproduce copyright material:

Photo credits: p.9 © Peter Horree/Alamy Stock Photo; **p.10** © The Image Works/TopFoto; **p.16** © jozef sedmak/Alamy Stock Photo; **p.17** ©olivierl/123RF; **p.21** © Fine Art Images/Heritage Images/Getty Images; **p.29** (top) © NASA/WMAP SCIENCE TEAM/SCIENCE PHOTO LIBRARY, (bottom) © RUSSELL KIGHTLEY/SCIENCE PHOTO LIBRARY; **p.30** © JOSE ANTONIO PENAS/SCIENCE PHOTO LIBRARY; **p.32** © nickolae/Fotolia; **p.33** © Anyka - Fotolia.com; **p.34** © Rob Cicchetti/123RF; **p.35** © TONY CAMACHO/SCIENCE PHOTO LIBRARY; **p.36** © Alexandr Mitiuc/Fotolia; **p.41** © sakkmesterke/123RF; **p.49** (top) © Jim West/Alamy Stock Photo, (bottom) © chungking/Fotolia; **p.57** © The Granger Collection/TopFoto; **p.64** (left) © Dimitrios - Fotolia.com, (right) © mdfiles/Fotolia; **p.70** © picsfive – Fotolia.com; **p.71** © Michalis Palis/Fotolia; **p.85** © Karel Miragaya/123RF; **p.86** (top) © luzitanija/123RF, (bottom) © Franck Boston/Fotolia; **p.89** © Timewatch Images/Alamy Stock Photo; **p.94** © Glasshouse Images/Alamy Stock Photo; **p.95** © viktor kunz/123RF; **p.98** © Paul Doyle/Alamy Stock Photo; **p.100** (left) © dpa picture alliance/Alamy Stock Photo, (right) © paul prescott - Fotolia.com; **p.114** © The Art Archive/Alamy Stock Photo; **p.115** © The Art Archive/Alamy Stock Photo; **p.116** © Godong/Universal Images Group/Getty Images; **p.117** © Angelo Giampiccolo – Fotolia; **p.127** © University of California Santa Cruz (Ron James Photography Collection); **p.129** © Barbara Bradley Hagerty/NPR; **p.130** © Victor de Schwanberg/Alamy Stock Photo; **p.132** (top) © Nikki Zalewski/Shutterstock, (bottom) © ArTo - Fotolia.com; **p.138** © The Art Archive/Alamy Stock Photo, **p.139** © Zvonimir Atletic/Alamy Stock Photo; **p.142** © PETER COSGROVE AP/Press Association Images

Images on pages 1, 145, 149 © Robert Spriggs/Fotolia; pages 5, 6, 26, 41 © rolffimages/Fotolia; pages 53, 54, 68, 76 © magann/Fotolia; pages 83, 84, 93, 103 © adimas/Fotolia; pages 111, 112, 125, 136 © ssilver/123RF

Acknowledgements: Course assessment and marking guidance content in pp 145–148 has been adapted from SQA course specification and support notes and marking instructions Copyright © Scottish Qualifications Authority. The exam-type questions are not derived from any SQA specimen or past papers.

Every effort has been made to trace all copyright holders, but if any have been inadvertently overlooked the Publishers will be pleased to make the necessary arrangements at the first opportunity.

Although every effort has been made to ensure that website addresses are correct at time of going to press, Hodder Gibson cannot be held responsible for the content of any website mentioned in this book. It is sometimes possible to find a relocated web page by typing in the address of the home page for a website in the URL window of your browser.

Hachette UK's policy is to use papers that are natural, renewable and recyclable products and made from wood grown in well-managed forests and other controlled sources. The logging and manufacturing processes are expected to conform to the environmental regulations of the country of origin.

Orders: please contact Bookpoint Ltd, 130 Park Drive, Milton Park, Abingdon, Oxon OX14 4SB. Telephone: +44 (0)1235 827827. Fax: +44 (0)1235 400454. Email education@bookpoint.co.uk Lines are open 9.00a.m.–5.00p.m., Monday to Saturday, with a 24-hour message answering service. Visit our website at www.hoddereducation.co.uk. Hodder Gibson can also be contacted directly at hoddergibson@hodder.co.uk.

© Joe Walker 2019

First published in 2016 © Joe Walker

This second edition published in 2019 by
Hodder Gibson, an imprint of Hodder Education
An Hachette UK Company
211 St Vincent Street
Glasgow, G2 5QY

Impression number 5 4 3 2 1
Year   2023 2022 2021 2020 2019

Cover photo © vovan - stock.adobe.com
Illustrations by Sarah Arnold Illustration
Typeset in India by Integra Software Services Ltd.
Printed in Italy

A catalogue record for this title is available from the British Library
ISBN: 978 1 5104 5780 5

Contents

Note to teachers

This book covers the 'Religious and Philosophical Questions' component of the Scottish Qualifications Authority course in Religious, Moral and Philosophical Studies (RMPS) at Higher level. It is designed to start young people thinking about religious and philosophical questions and developing their own beliefs as a result. Like many topic areas in RMPS, each topic, in fact each chapter, could be a book on its own so I have, as always, aimed to keep it all relatively simple while hopefully providing enough detail to open up these complex and interesting areas of discussion. As you know, many of these are very sensitive topics for some, and viewpoints and beliefs around many of these issues run deep and discussions can be heated.

I have strived very carefully to avoid taking any 'sides' in any of the debates and discussions – that is neither my job nor yours. Our role is to provide the contexts for thinking for young people, encouraging depth, reflection and analysis of the areas for discussion, and to support them in developing their own views so that they can build their own world view to support them in their own lives.

As ever, I have followed the structure of the course as set out by the SQA. In addition, I hope that occasional forays into other areas of interest might support inspiring teaching and learning, and allow for some element of personalisation and choice for young people even though they are following a specific National Qualification (NQ) course. The availability of so many sources of information these days is a great boost for teaching and learning, but it can also sometimes be overwhelming, so hopefully this book can set learners off in helpful directions and start to make sense of all that is out there.

In terms of course content, I have tried to include some variety here but for some topics I have deliberately limited the text to 'classical' arguments as well as focusing specifically on largely Western European and Christian contexts. There is nothing to prohibit learners from studying creation, evolution, Big Bang, the problem of suffering and evil, miracles and so on in the context of any religion of their choosing, but to make things manageable in this book I have focused on a largely Judaeo-Christian context, with opportunities in the 'Investigate' section for learners to extend their learning across other religions and belief groups.

I have included exam-type questions and various assessment activities but, as always, please ensure that you are following the latest SQA advice and guidance in relation to coursework and SQA question structures.

I have tried to give a specifically Scottish flavour where I can – hopefully not to the point of parochialism but in a way which resonates with young people in a Scottish context. Some of the topics don't exactly lend themselves to a laugh-a-minute approach, but I have tried to keep things light without being flippant, and humorous without being disrespectful. You will find some repetition in this book, for which I apologise. The current SQA course has a lot of overlapping areas of study and I have assumed that most learners will focus only on one topic. Where there is repetition, I have endeavoured to keep the text fresh.

I hope this is all of use to you.

Note to learners

Congratulations on choosing RMPS. You will find yourself in the middle of a subject which is right at the heart of the big questions facing the world today. In fact, in some ways these questions are exactly what make us human. The purpose of this book is to help you think through these big questions and arrive at your own conclusions. Try not to believe something just because someone says so and ask yourself questions as you read this book. You won't find my opinion in this book because what I think about these topics really isn't of any importance to anyone but me. So develop and extend your own beliefs and values and put them into action in positive ways. People of my generation (I'm 56 now and started writing RME/RMPS textbooks when I was 29) sometimes say things like 'The future is in the hands of our young people.' Sometimes they mean 'Oh dear, what will happen now?!' And sometimes, like me, they mean 'That's good – the world is in safe hands.' I know it's corny and cheesy, but you really are the future and I've worked with young people long enough to trust that you know what you're doing with it. So enjoy this course and let it help you to develop as a human being so that you can make the world a better place. There's no need to panic – I'm not handing that job on to you just yet, but it's getting ever closer ... Making the world a better place is the responsibility of all of us, no matter what age we are.

Religious and philosophical questions

1

Once upon a time there was a worm. The worm wriggles through the soil each day doing whatever it is that worms do with soil. All day long its little segmented and slithery body – which is about 90% water – moves through the soil. It wriggles, it writhes and it moves around. One day it might even mate with another worm and produce little cocoons out of which little baby worms will emerge. These tiny little worms will wriggle through the soil each day doing whatever it is that worms do with soil. All day long their segmented and slithery little bodies will move through the soil ... By now you may be hoping for more from our little wormy chum, but sadly this tale has little to offer. No one really knows what goes through a worm's mind, such as it is; no one really knows if anything much goes through a worm's mind – but all day long the little worm wriggles through the soil ...

I'm very sorry indeed if this little story is boring you beyond all comprehension and I hope you're not too troubled by this start to your course. Perhaps you are already asleep. But I'm afraid there isn't a whole lot else to say about this little worm. Of course, if this little worm could communicate with us then things would be very different, and I might have a wonderful tale to tell – but for the moment, there's nothing more than this little worm wriggling through the soil each day doing whatever it is that worms do with soil ...

What are religious and philosophical questions?

Now, of course, we might be greatly underestimating worm-power and perhaps the average worm has an incredibly active mind, but as far as we know … it doesn't. Humans, on the other hand, generally ask deep and searching questions right from the point at which they can communicate: young children are forever asking 'Why?' And even when they have an answer they often continue to ask 'Why?' again and again.

Philosophical questions are sometimes referred to as the 'big questions' or 'ultimate questions'. They are questions about meaning, about value, and about purpose in life. Some people might say that the ability to think about, ask and consider these questions is the thing that makes us uniquely human. Maybe humans are meaning-seeking creatures who want to know why things are the way they are and what this means for each of us. So perhaps in studying this course you are engaging in something which identifies you as a human being – a creature uniquely placed to consider its place in the universe, communicate with others about that and follow that thinking through with action in your life.

Philosophy is about thinking – about reason, logic and about constructing and analysing arguments and viewpoints. Philosophers ask the big questions and think about how we might answer them, as well as what these questions mean for us. There are many different kinds of philosophical viewpoint but all share the common feature that they are – essentially – thinking about thinking. Philosophy aims to use reason and argument to arrive at possible answers to the big questions – and where answers are impossible, to get as close to an answer as it is possible to do.

Religion is a complicated concept. It involves a great many factors which are social, psychological, practical and historical among other things. Religion involves belief and practice and may be based on faith – though this is not always the case. Religious people, too, use reason and argument and logic sometimes to arrive at answers. Sometimes they also base their answers on faith – believing in the absence of evidence, or in the presence of contradictory evidence, perhaps even when reason might point in another direction entirely.

The connection between religion and philosophy is also complex. Religions have philosophies which are part of what they are based upon. Many philosophers are religious. Religion can be examined using philosophy as a tool of investigation and, of course, philosophy and religion have considered many of the same questions for a long, long time.

Can these religious and philosophical questions be answered?

Some people get a little annoyed with some of the religious and philosophical questions you will examine in this book. They think that because there are no immediate answers – or, in their opinion, any chance that there will ever be any answers – there's not much point in discussing them. You'll have to develop your own view of that, but think of it this way. Choose your favourite sport. Imagine someone said that there was no point in engaging in your chosen sport because eventually it finishes – so there's no point in starting a football match because it will be over after 90 minutes. That wouldn't make sense and you would probably tell them it's not just the end result that matters – it's the whole process of doing the sport. So take the question 'Does God exist?' Perhaps there will never be an answer to that question, so does that mean we should never ask it or think about it? Maybe in asking and discussing that question we will learn a little more about ourselves and about others – understand ourselves, others, and the world in which we live. Now what can be wrong with that? Some people think that considering these questions helps develop our thinking skills and so helps us to deal with many more questions in life and, as a result, live a better, more fulfilled life. At the end of the day, only you can decide if asking and trying to answer these questions makes any sense.

How do I know if I've got it right?

The answer in this case is quite tricky. Many of these questions may not have a 'right' or 'wrong' answer – in fact, what makes something right or wrong is a religious and philosophical question in itself! Some people will, of course, claim that there is a 'right' and 'wrong' answer to many of these questions but you will have to make up your own mind about that – after all, that's the whole point of this course.

Why are many of these questions so controversial?

Many of the questions you will examine in this course provoke strong opinions and heated argument. For most people, what they think or believe is very important to them and they like to defend these thoughts and beliefs. Sometimes defending your thoughts and beliefs is done through argument and discussion, and sometimes in less desirable ways. People feel strongly about things and can be sensitive to their thoughts, beliefs and way of life being somehow under attack in these discussions – they may 'fight' back in some way or other. This shows that thoughts, viewpoints, opinions and beliefs can be very important to people and so are very carefully guarded against 'attack' by others. This book will take no 'sides' about any of these questions – its aim is to provide you with the basic information and let you think through the questions for yourself. What conclusions you reach are entirely up to you.

Facts, figures, opinions ... life skills

Throughout this course, as you deal with these complex questions, you will come across many things which are facts or are claimed to be facts. You will examine opinions and viewpoints and consider beliefs. You will try to separate out claims about reason and logic. You will consider, reflect upon, analyse and evaluate, construct and de-construct arguments and assertions. You will investigate, synthesise, report on, talk about, discuss, present ... These are all key skills you will need in life in a variety of contexts. So, no matter what the topic you're examining, you will be developing important skills for learning, life and work. Importantly, too, you will be thinking about your own responses to these questions and so you will be building your own identity as you grow, mature and develop – and you will do this long after this course; in fact, throughout the rest of your life. Thinking about these questions will help you to make sense of life, to make sense of others and, perhaps most importantly, to make sense of yourself.

Pre-course thinking

Before you start your coursework, you should use the following questions for open class discussion and debate. These will get you thinking about religious and philosophical questions no matter what topic you are studying in the course. There are many links between these big questions anyway. You do not need to discuss all these questions but, with help from your teacher, select a few to focus on to start you off.

- Does life have a 'purpose'?
- Is religion still an important feature in today's world?
- Is there a point to philosophy?
- Is there such a thing as God or gods?
- What beliefs do people have about God or gods?
- Where do our beliefs come from?
- How closely are our beliefs linked to our upbringing, and where and when we live?
- What other factors influence our beliefs?
- How do we judge if a religion is true?
- Can we ever know if a religion is true?
- Should we question people's beliefs?
- What is faith?
- How do we work out if something is true or not?
- Do we need evidence for anything we believe?
- How did the universe begin?
- Does the world around us suggest the existence of a creator?
- How did life on Earth begin?
- Is there anything special about human beings?
- Why do bad things happen?
- Does the existence of evil call into question the existence of God or gods?
- What is suffering and why do people suffer?
- Does suffering have value?
- Are humans completely free?
- Are human choices and actions within our control?
- How important is human freedom?
- Have miracles ever happened and do they still happen today?

ORIGINS: WERE
THE UNIVERSE
AND LIFE
CREATED?

The Tarpatu people of New Sasaland believe that this is how the universe began ...

At the start there was nothing – although this was also something – but not as we know it. Then, from this nothing-something came the Neratu. This can only be explained by likening it to something we know about. The closest thing to it today might be a potato. So this potato appeared from the nothing-something and in the process lost its nothingness, leaving behind only its somethingness. Its nothingness has not gone entirely, for most of the universe as we know it today is composed of it.

So the great potato sprouted eyes – as potatoes tend to do. Now these eyes became shoots, then stalks and stems and leaves and flowers – on a truly cosmic scale. As the Neratu grew, its growth reached into all of the nothingness and filled it with a multitude of somethings. These took new shapes and forms – liquids and gases, fluid and solid, energy and light, and trasua – of which we know little, even today.

As the Neratu grew it soon came to be unrecognisable as the universal potato it had once been, and all its shoots became other things – with no memory of what they had once been and no memory of the first great potato which became all things.

Perhaps in the end, it will all result in a great mash, or splinter into an infinite number of chips ... Who can say?

From the Neratu all things came. What their end will be no one knows.

Did something once sow the great Neratu? Was there something before the Neratu? What remains of the Neratu now? None can know ...

Talk Point

How would you respond if one of the Tarpatu people told you that 'this story is 100 per cent, completely true'?

Creation stories around the world

Hopefully you have guessed that the Tarpatu's creation story is completely fictional – although perhaps it might be nice to think of the universe beginning in the form of a big cheery potato. Around the world and throughout history there have been many versions of the creation of the universe. In many of these stories the universe simply comes into being through some process or other; in other stories there is something or someone which sets it all in motion. Most often this great being, person or entity exists without explanation – or with the explanation that this being has always been there and requires no beginning. For some reason, known only to this being, he/she/it decides to make other things and goes about creating the universe. Everything which exists today is then thought of as the result of the creative action of this great being. Sometimes, parts of the body of this great being become physical features of the universe itself; other times the great being remains separate from the universe it creates. In some stories, this being is imagined as human-like – or at least recognisable in some way as something living that we are familiar with, just on a huge cosmic scale. In other stories, this being is a force or power, an energy form which has no features and is not physical in the way we understand it today. For many, these stories are considered to be literally true. They happened exactly as written (or spoken) – they are history. For others, the stories are pointers to something which really happened, but which was far too complex for us ever to understand and so it is approached as a piece of poetry – a way of putting into words something which is beyond words. There are many creation stories across the world. From China comes the story of a great cosmic egg filled with the being Pan Ku. In the Pacific Islands, creation is brought about by the great god Tangaroa. In the world of the Inuit, the story is told of the greedy and eventually fingerless Sedna, from whose drowned body came all things …

Some questions raised by these stories

If any of these stories is completely and literally true – meaning accurate historical fact – then right away we have a few problems:

▶ How can they all be true at the same time? Surely if one is true then another is false. Is one a lie and the other truth? Is one an accurate explanation and another a misunderstanding?

▶ What if all or part of one story contradicts another (or even includes contradictions of itself)? What if one story said that everything was created by a being and another that everything simply came into existence itself? How can both be true?

▶ How did we come to know about the story since the only being around at the time was the creator him/her/itself? In many of the stories, rational thinking beings take some time to appear on the scene. Did the great creator sit down with one of them one day and share with that person the story of creation so that the person could hand it on? How can we be sure that this person handed on the story accurately and that his/her/their descendants did the same throughout the rest of history?

▶ And, of course, perhaps the biggest problem is this: if there was a being which created everything and so is the origin of everything, what was the origin of that being? In what way does it make sense to say that everything required a beginning except the thing which brought everything into existence? More of that later.

Responses to creation stories

So how do we respond to the many creation stories which are believed around the world today?

▶ **They are all true.** Maybe all these stories are true in some way. Imagine a beautiful painting. You could describe this painting in a story or in a poem. You could write a song about it. You could describe, in scientific terms, the paints used and the percentages of one colour as opposed to another. You could measure the painting and describe it in numbers. All these ways of 'explaining' the painting would be perfectly true, but different. So perhaps all the creation stories in the world today are true – just different ways of communicating the same events.

▶ **One of them is true and all the others are not.** We have to face this possibility. Perhaps one story is accurate and all the others are not. Perhaps all the others were just made up to provide some entertainment around the fire on a cold night. Perhaps the other stories were made up to discredit the one true story. Perhaps the other stories are the result of the poor memory of storytellers through the years. Maybe there was one true story which everyone agreed on, and over the years bits of it were forgotten or changed by accident or on purpose, so that after a long time they turned into what appear to be completely different stories.

▶ **There is some truth in all of them.** Maybe the outward features of the story are less important than the truths which lie behind it. Perhaps all the stories contain some truth, but are ways of telling the 'one true story' in different ways which are suitable for people hearing the story at different times and in different contexts.

▶ **The stories are 'meaning-makers'.** Perhaps humans are meaning-seeking creatures and we have a built-in need to make sense of things – we need to build a story to help us understand. For example, imagine that you hear that your friend was put out of his maths class by his teacher. Right away you will probably ask a whole series of questions: 'What did he do? What did he say? What did the maths teacher do? What happened next? Have his parents been told? What did they do?' All of your questions point to your need to understand the story – to make one kind of meaning out of the events. Perhaps, as we experience the world around us, we constantly need to make sense of it – and we do this through story.

Talk Point

Are some creation stories more 'believable' than others? What might make them so?

The Judaeo-Christian creation story

There are many creation stories but for this course we will focus on the Judaeo-Christian story. While this is often referred to as the Christian creation story (by Christians, of course), it first appeared in the scriptures of Judaism, and there is a version accepted within Islam too. As this story has one specific creator, we will use this as a focus for our understanding. The story begins with nothingness, then the divine being creates everything through a series of creative actions, with the final act of creation being human beings. In Judaism, this being is referred to as the great 'I am', with the Hebrew name 'Yahweh' – a name which is so powerful it is not said aloud; instead is uttered the word 'Adonai' (my Lord) or Lord. This being has become referred to most commonly as God. (In Judaism, this is often written as G-d to reflect the importance and power of the name.) Christians refer to this being as God and Muslims call him Allah. Across these three religions, it is understood that this being is the same being – and for the purposes of this book we shall simply refer to him as God. While we're at it, we will also refer to God as 'him' and 'he'. This is not sexism – it simply reflects the usual approach in these three religions, although there are religious people who are quite happy to refer to God as 'her' and 'she'. When 'him' and 'he' are used in relation to God they are often written as 'Him' and 'He' but we will not use that form in this book. Finally, we will use 'God' rather than 'god' as this will show clearly that we are talking about the Jewish/Christian/Muslim God and not other gods from other religions. Hope that's all nice and clear …

The Judaeo-Christian story can be found in the book of Genesis (the word means 'origin') – perhaps unsurprisingly in the first few pages of Chapter 1. The story is generally accepted as follows:

1 There is nothing. Everything is formless and desolate.
2 God decides to make something out of nothing.
3 He creates light and separates day from night, and land from sea.
4 He then adds life forms to land.
5 Next he makes celestial bodies – the Sun, the Moon, stars and all that.
6 Then he adds further life forms to the seas and creates more land-based life.
7 Finally he forms human beings as the pinnacle of his creation. These human beings are made 'in his own likeness' (or 'image'). In some translations of the scripture it says that 'human beings will resemble us'. There are many different views about what this might mean.
8 Then a well-deserved rest is in order.

The timescale for the story was stated in the scriptures as six days, with the seventh a day of rest. Bear in mind that the word 'days' might have many different meanings.

Creation – the early humans

The creation of human beings was specifically explained in the second chapter of the book of Genesis. (In Islam, reference to the creation story occurs in a number of places throughout the Quran (Koran) and there are some differences in detail about creation between Islam and the Judaeo-Christian version.) In the book of Genesis, God takes soil from the earth and forms a man – Adam – into whom he breathes 'life-giving breath'. At this point, God tells man that he is in charge and can do anything – except eat from a particular tree. Deciding that man is lonely, he makes a woman – Eve. Now everything is perfect and Adam and Eve live the perfect life.

However, in this garden of perfection there is a snake who persuades Eve to eat from the forbidden tree, and she, in turn, persuades Adam to do so as well. God is not at all pleased and punishes them for their disobedience by expelling them from the garden. Things very quickly turn unpleasant in the story from this point on. Adam and Eve have two sons – Cain and Abel – and soon the world's first murder is committed as Cain kills Abel. The motive for this murder is Cain's unhappiness at God's acceptance of Abel's offering of a lamb, having rejected Cain's offering. Cain and his wife (no explanation is given about where Cain's wife came from) have a son, Enoch.

Adam lived to be 930 years old and a long list of descendants follow, ending in the three sons of the 500-year-old Noah. In between this, 'supernatural beings' (or 'sons of God' or 'sons of the gods') took human girls for themselves, resulting in the birth of 'giants'. According to Genesis, human behaviour eventually became so wicked that God decided he would start all over again. He sent a flood to wipe out everything except for one good man – Noah and his family – who survived in a great boat along with two of every species. Noah's three sons – Shem, Ham and Japheth – left the boat with their wives after the flood and became the ancestors of all humans on Earth. Humans then repopulated the Earth – and life goes on as normal.

Talk Point

What questions does the story of the early humans in Genesis raise for you?

Origins of the story

So this story can be found in the scriptures of Judaism, Christianity and Islam – but how did it come to be remembered today?

Talk Point

How do you think this creation story found its way into the scriptures of Judaism, Christianity and Islam?

Judaism/Christianity

The Judaeo-Christian story may have two possible origins. First there is the divine communication origin. This is the view that the story was communicated directly from God to humans. This might then have been passed down through the ages by word of mouth until it was eventually captured in writing, or spoken by God directly to the writers of the Jewish scriptures, who wrote it down immediately to be captured in writing and passed down that way. This origin of the story would suggest that the story we have now is absolutely as it happened, because it is as God himself described it – and he should know.

Another possibility is the oral transmission origin, that somehow the story was passed down through time, person to person. Perhaps parts of it were written down – possibly by different people at different times, drawing upon different memories of the story passed down. Eventually a version was agreed that has become the story we have today. Of course, this way of passing down the story could mean that bits were forgotten or amended as the story was passed down – and so perhaps the story we have is not as pure as it could be. (Of course, God might have made sure that each part of the story was passed down accurately until it was captured in writing.)

Responses to the Judaeo-Christian story

Literalist/Creationist understandings

We will discuss these in detail in the next chapter, but for the moment it is enough to say that some religious people accept the scriptural accounts of the creation as literally true – that they happened exactly as the scriptures describe them. They accept this as a matter of faith – which means that they can accept anything which might seem complicated – or, in some people's opinion, 'far-fetched' – about the stories. They believe in an all-powerful creator who could create the universe exactly as the scriptures describe it being created – end of discussion. This also applies to the story of the first humans – one man and woman and their descendants. There was a great worldwide flood and only Noah and his family survived.

Creationists believe in the literal truth of the scriptural accounts of creation. Some base this on faith alone – arguing that if it is in the scriptures then it is true as written and there's no real need for any further discussion. Others go beyond this and argue that not only is it true because it is in the scriptures, but it is true because there is scientific evidence to support the scriptural account. These people take creationism further to what has become known as creation science or intelligent design – again, more detail on that later.

Metaphorical understandings

Some religious people believe that there is some truth in the creation story but that it is not meant to be a historically true and scientifically accurate account of what happened. It is a story which is designed to convey meaning, not a scientific textbook. This means that they think of aspects of the story as representative of other things, as allegory, metaphor and simile – ways of pointing to a truth which is too complex to explain in any meaningful way for anyone to understand. So perhaps Adam and Eve were just a representative story, and there were other men and women in existence too, or perhaps 'Adam' means mankind and 'Eve' womankind. Perhaps the story is just a fable to explain the falling out between God and his creation.

'Scientific' responses

We have to be careful about the use of the words 'science' and 'scientific' here. Many scientists are also religious people and believe that the Judaeo-Christian creation story is true – some quite literally, some more as metaphor. There can be many reasons why scientists such as these might believe the creation story, and it would be inaccurate to say that all scientists reject the story. What we can say is that for many, scientific evidence calls into question many aspects of the creation story and throws doubt upon it being literally true. And, of course, for many, scientific evidence completely contradicts any possible reading of the creation story as a literally true account of events. However, there are many shades of opinion here and we need to be careful about thinking that religious belief is always in one corner and scientific evidence in another. There is also a position known as 'Scientific Materialism' which is important to be aware of. This position rejects religious explanations and holds that physical realities are all that can be said to exist.

What does the Judaeo-Christian creation story imply about a creator?

Some creation stories have no role for any creator. Instead, cosmic processes do the work. For others, there is a limited role for a creator which is summed up in what we might think of as a cosmic drama. In others, such as the Judaeo-Christian story, there is a central role for a creator – one supernatural and super-powerful being who brings into existence something other than himself. What does the creation story suggest about this creator?

Talk Point

What does the Judaeo-Christian creation story say to you about the possible nature and existence of God?

The creator is all-powerful/all-knowing

To create everything from nothing requires a being which is unimaginably powerful. Such a being could have created any kind of universe. The fact that he created this one is just what it is. For some, this raises questions. Why did the creator create this universe in the way he did? Had there been any universes before this? Will this one end and be replaced? Why did the creator make the decision to create it in the first place?

For some, the universe is an amazing, beautiful place full of wonder – pointing to a benevolent creator. For others, the universe is a place of unimaginable violence and power – pointing to a creator who might value violence and power more than we would like him to. There is one interesting difficulty with this concept. As far as the creation of human life on Earth is concerned, the story is clear that the creator changed his mind (and perhaps did not expect certain things to happen). He decided to wipe out all life on Earth because of its wickedness, saving only Noah (and his lucky family). Does this suggest that he got it wrong when making humans, or that he allowed them too much freedom? And was his solution of worldwide destruction of all life a proportionate response? Also, did God not foresee Adam and Eve's disobedience? And when he rejected Cain's offering, was he unaware of the effect this might have on Cain and its tragic consequences? Perhaps all of these questions can be overlooked if the story is a human story to explain something otherwise inexplicable – but, if not, perhaps it raises some very difficult questions about the all-powerful/all-knowing nature of God.

The creator is separate from or totally involved in creation

This is a complex one. Some people believe that the creator created all things and then left it all to run as it did. In a way, he switched on the machinery of the universe and then stepped back, having nothing more to do with it. If this is so, why did he create it in the first place? Why would he have made something and then simply left it to its own devices? For some, this is quite a depressing idea because they would say this makes God a remote and unfeeling being who is not really interested in anything after he sets it in motion.

Other people believe the opposite – that the creator is intimately involved with all creation, and always has been. He sees all and is part of all. He experiences along with us and cares for us – sharing our highs and lows in life – and the life of all things everywhere.

For some, different questions are raised by the relationship between creator and created. Some think of everything as God and God as everything; others think of God as a separate being entirely – outside of space and time. But if he is outside of space and time, where and when is he? Can he be in the past, present and future all at the same time? As you see, it is far from simple!

Creation points to the creator

Some think that the universe gives us clues about the nature of the creator; others wonder why we need to be cosmic detectives, investigating the nature of the creator but never quite solving the case. Why, they might ask, does the creator not simply reveal himself to us – would this rob us of some mystery, or maybe answer some deep questions for us? If the creator does care for his creation, what is the need for him to keep himself hidden from us? Would anyone who cared for anyone else really want to keep themselves hidden from them all through their life? Why would they do so?

If creation does tell us something about the creator, what is it telling us? Importantly, is it telling us that the creator is the God believed in by Jewish people, Christians and Muslims? Some religious people think of God as having a shape and a form – perhaps quite a human one – while others think of God more as energy and power. For Jewish people and Muslims, of course, God is one being – completely alone and without equal – while for Christians, God is three: Father, Son and Holy Spirit.

There are also some possible difficulties about what creation stories tell us about a creator. Some people might consider the universe to be a violent struggle for survival, where only the strongest survive. What does this say about its creator?

The creator is uncreated

For some people, this is one of the most difficult points. If the creator needs no beginning, why does creation? The 'First Cause' argument, proposed at one point by Thomas Aquinas, states that everything needs to be caused by something else. However, because this would mean that we would go back through time infinitely with cause after cause after cause (and Aquinas thought this did not make sense), there must have – at one point – been a first cause to cause all the other causes. Aquinas argued that by definition, a first cause such as this must be God – who therefore must need no cause.

Of course, there are some difficulties with this argument. If there had to be a first cause, why could the universe not cause itself to be created in the first place? If God requires no cause, then why must the universe? Even if a first cause was a divine being, why does it need to be God? It could have been a quite different being, or a committee of gods or some different creature entirely. Why does it need to be the God of the Judaeo-Christian belief?

The creator has communicated something about himself through the creation of humans

Humans are made in the 'image of God' so there is something about us which points to God. Is this telling us something about how God looks, or how he thinks and feels? Do humans share something of the nature of God – and, if so, what? Does God have any kind of need for humans and, if so, what does this say about him? If humans are the stars of the creation story, do the actions of some humans in the world today – and throughout history – call into question the design abilities of God?

Religious responses to the role of a creator

There are a number of possible religious responses when thinking about the existence and actions of a creator.

▶ Based on faith alone, religious people may argue that the universe was created as their scriptures describe it. They would argue that the universe requires a creator, and that the size of such a task requires an all-powerful divine being which can only be God. They would argue that such a God is their God because their scriptures say so and for a number of other reasons as well, including their experience about what they believe to be true. Their view is that the universe needs a first cause and that cause must be God.

▶ Many would add that in their opinion there is plenty of evidence for the existence of a creator. The design, order and structure of the universe could only be explained by its being created by an intelligent, powerful and benevolent being with our best interests at heart. This is going beyond faith to use reason to support their belief. In short, the existence of the universe as it is today is reasonable cause to believe that it was brought about by God. In their view, aspects of their own lives today (or those of others) can be considered as evidence of the existence of a divine creator.

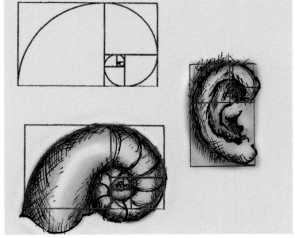

▶ Many religious people accept the literal truth of creation stories and can accept what might seem to be anomalies in the stories (such as where Cain's wife came from). They would argue that we cannot and need not have answers for everything in the scriptures and that we simply have to accept what they say at face value. Religious belief is about faith – which means that you cannot choose to believe some aspects of the scriptures and ignore others.

▶ Some religious people argue that there is good scientific evidence to support scriptural creation stories. Such creation scientists, or supporters of intelligent design, use science to support their beliefs that the universe was created by God and that events such as the worldwide flood happened as described.

- Other religious people treat the creation stories as metaphors which point to truths, but which are not to be accepted as literal truths. This means that issues such as the scientific truth of the worldwide flood, for example, do not need to be considered, since the story is a myth designed to communicate meaning, not historical fact. This means that the existence of a creator is not challenged by any apparent issues in the scriptural accounts of creation.

So religious people may use faith alone as a reason for believing in a creator – or they may use a mixture of both faith and reason.

Non-religious responses to the role of a creator

There are a number of reasons why those who have no religious belief reject the view that the universe was created.

- Lack of evidence. For most non-religious people, there is simply no evidence to support the existence of a divine creator. There is no evidence from what we know of the origins of the universe and life on Earth, as well as no evidence that such a being exists today. In their view, to believe anything requires evidence – measurable, objective and scientific evidence – and they think this cannot be found to support the existence of a creator.
- Non-religious people would also argue that there is no evidence to support scriptural accounts of creation and that, in fact, the evidence points the other way. The age of the Earth, a worldwide flood, the survival of two of every species – there is, in their opinion, no evidence to support these and much evidence to cast very serious doubt on their truth. In their view, creation science and intelligent design are not scientific in the way that they understand science to be.
- Non-religious people would argue that we need to take scriptural accounts for what they are – myths from a specific time and place. There were many flood stories in the ancient Near East (the area now commonly referred to as the Middle East), such as in the *Epic of Gilgamesh*. Why should the Judaeo-Christian story be anything more than just another of these fables? Besides, even if any aspect of the Judaeo-Christian creation story was true, it still gives us a confusing picture of God. For example, God's unexplained rejection of Cain's offering which led to the murder of Abel – did God not foresee this?
- Many non-religious people argue that it is unreasonable to assume the creation of the universe by a creator. If the creator did not need to be created, why did the universe need to be created? To some people this simply does not make sense. Even if there was a need for a creator, why did it have to be any specific god? Why the God of the Judaeo-Christian tradition? In fact, they might argue, the universe is based on struggle, violence and power where only the fittest survive – so what does this say about God?

So for non-religious people, the role of a creator is an unlikely one because it is unsupported (and possibly contradicted) by evidence, and it is based on very poor reasoning.

I believe in the literal truth of the Bible, and to do so I need to do no more than read the story. The universe was created by God in six days. That's six periods of twenty-four hours. The Bible tells us the order of creation and how God's relationship with the first man and woman went wrong because of their disobedience. Yes, it tells us that God punished them by exiling them from the garden of perfection, and that he annihilated their descendants in a great flood. Their wickedness brought this about and God is a God of justice …

I believe in the literal truth of the Bible. It is God's word and so it is true. But something being true does not mean that you have to accept it as it is written. I believe that God created everything in six days – but I don't need to have big discussions about what 'day' means. I believe that God created Adam and Eve – but I don't need to worry if this means two people or two thousand. I believe there was a flood and I believe that people were wicked – but I don't need to believe that everyone died everywhere and that a boat took two of every species …

I am a Bible-believing Christian – but you need to be clear about what that means. I believe in the fact that God created everything, but the biblical story has to be understood as something which is linked to a particular time and place. I believe that the first humans disobeyed God, but that doesn't mean I need to believe in a talking snake and a very dodgy piece of fruit …

I am a Christian. I believe God created the universe and life on Earth. I believe the Bible points to truths about this, but I don't believe it is scientific fact. It is a myth with meaning. It helped people to understand in times past but nowadays we can see it for what it is – a story. Does this challenge my faith? It does not need to …

We have become so tied up in questions about the literal truth of the biblical stories that we have lost sight of what our faith is for. What good does it do to have endless discussions about whether six days means six periods of twenty-four hours? What good does it do to go looking for the remains of Noah's ark? My faith is something to be lived today – through serving others and living the life which God wants for me. Such discussions are all very well for some but for me they are irrelevant: too much time is wasted on thinking about them when at the end of the day it is all a matter of faith. Live a good life, serve God and serve others – don't waste your time on pointless discussions …

Responses to the creation story

We have now examined some basic responses to the Judaeo-Christian creation story (which we will now refer to as the 'biblical story') from religious and non-religious people. Now we will home in a little more on different views about this story held by religious people and look at some responses to them. There are two main religious positions but each of these positions has a number of different shades of viewpoint within it.

Talk Point

How do you respond to the viewpoints above

Literal interpretations

This means believing that the biblical story is completely true in all respects. Six days means six days and Adam and Eve were tempted by a snake. Everything else which happens in the Bible happened as described – literally.

At this point it is important to say that some religious people think you must accept the literal truth of the biblical story to call yourself a religious person, while others would completely disagree with this view.

Those who understand the creation stories literally might argue that the key strength here is that you simply believe. There is no need for gathering evidence, looking for proof or studying science. Such people might argue that understanding the biblical stories literally is a sign of faith, and supports a life based on trust and certainty rather than doubt and uncertainty.

On the other hand, a possible weakness of understanding the stories literally might be that by doing so you are ignoring the evidence. This makes it complicated when there are different views of the stories – since it could all just come down to 'you believe this, I believe that'.

Metaphorical interpretations

This means that the biblical story contains truths but that these truths are wrapped up in metaphor, simile, analogy and other ways of communicating reality which are about pointing to truths through story. This means that aspects of the story may be communicated through symbolism or other literary techniques. For example, 'Adam' might stand for all mankind, the 'forbidden tree' might stand for some knowledge which only God should have and the 'snake' might stand for the temptation of an enquiring mind.

A possible strength of understanding the stories metaphorically is that you can then deal more easily with apparent contradictions and things which otherwise might not make sense. For example, avoiding the need to answer questions such as where did Adam and Eve's son find a partner with whom he could have children?

However, one possible weakness of understanding the stories metaphorically is that you would then have to choose which elements you thought were literally true and which were not. On what basis might you reach this decision? This has the potential to become a rather confusing muddle of 'that's true, but that's not'. Some might also argue that not accepting the stories as literally true brings into question your faith.

Religious explanations: literal explanations

Often the science presented in support of literal understandings of creation stories is complex for ordinary people to understand – and, of course, some claim that it is not science. However, in assessing the credibility of literal accounts of the creation story and those who believe in it literally (whom we will refer to as 'the claimants') perhaps we should take into account the following:

▸ What does the claimant have to gain from expressing their views? (bias/neutrality)
▸ What qualifies the claimant to express their views – for example, what scientific or other authority do they have? (authority)
▸ How far has the claimant recognised and taken into account any evidence which contradicts their views? (confirmation bias/appropriate scientific method)
▸ How did the claimant arrive at their views? (source of their belief – scientific or religious?)

It is important to point out that all of these questions could also be asked about those who reject literal interpretations of creation stories.

Explanations based on biblical creationism and intelligent design

One understanding of creationism takes the view that the Bible is revealed truth and so is not there to be doubted. God is all-powerful and the creation of the universe and life on it is completely beyond our understanding – therefore the only way to explain it is in the form of a story. It is really not our place to question or doubt the story. God gave us the Bible and so we must assume that he wanted to tell us about the creation of the universe in this way. Our role is to accept in faith the story as told and get on with our lives as religious people. Adam and Eve were the first humans and they disobeyed God which resulted in a set of consequences. For creationists, there is little point in discussing the biblical story – it is there to be accepted and believed as it is written. That is what faith means. They believe the Bible is divinely inspired so is true in every word.

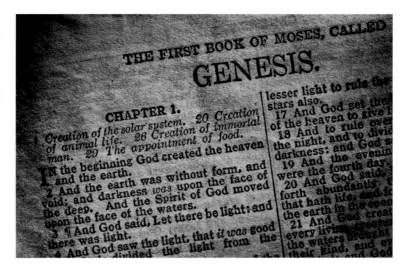

A slightly different version of biblical creationism takes the view that while the Bible is completely true and points to God as creator, a religious person can still 'read meaning into' the story. For example, while there was an actual Adam and Eve, this is just one story about two representative people – among many whom God created at first. Their story stands for all humanity – and its disobedience – so while they were real, they were not the only two humans on Earth at the time. Similarly, there was a flood as described in the story but it was not a worldwide flood in the sense that water covered all the Earth. Instead, it covered just the world as the writers of the time knew it. (This could have been the area around the Mediterranean Sea, which was thought to constitute the whole world at the time.) So, this kind of creationist believes that the Bible is divinely inspired and therefore true in every word, but also allows for some interpretation of those words to help them make sense of some of its possible loopholes.

Some creationists do not take into account any scientific claims about the origin of the universe or life on Earth. In their view, the biblical story is evidence enough and they do not need scientific support. Nor do they think that science has a role to play in questioning faith. Other creationists challenge scientific claims which seem to contradict the events written about in the Bible and others still go even further and try to find scientific evidence to support their creationist views.

Possible strengths of explanations based on biblical creationism and intelligent design

Those who support a biblical creationism or intelligent design approach might argue that accepting the stories as literally true is an act of faith. It avoids any need for complex and possibly quite convoluted arguments. You do not need to understand complex scientific principles, or be able to weigh up potentially very difficult scientific evidence. For those who propose this view, it upholds their faith, in that they can believe regardless of any contradictory scientific evidence, and/or without having to take it into account at all. For them, perhaps, the Bible is evidence enough, as is their understanding that the complexity and beauty of the universe and of life itself points to the truth of the biblical stories. They might further argue that it is not our place to call into question divinely-inspired scriptural accounts of the origins of the universe and of life. For supporters of this view, God is an all-powerful being who can act in any way he chooses, and it is our role to simply accept that. Some would argue that taking this approach is the most elegant and simplest approach, in line with a life based on faith.

Possible weaknesses of explanations based on biblical creationism and intelligent design

One possible weakness of biblical creationism is that some might consider it to be a 'closed circle' of belief. In other words, 'the biblical story is true because I believe in the truth of the Bible'. This means there is no option of further discussion because the person's mind is closed to the possibility that the Bible is anything other than the truth of the matter. Such people will give authority to the biblical story and reject other creation stories because they believe the Bible to be true. This is especially likely to be the case where the creationist accepts the literal truth of every word. Connected to this is the view that creation must have been by God because only God could do such a thing. This, too, is seen as a circular argument because it claims that God's actual existence is proved by a need for his existence.

For creationists who are prepared to write a little meaning into the stories, one possible weakness might be that they are simply choosing what to believe and what not to believe. For example, once you are prepared to accept that six days might be any time period, why not go further and question other aspects of the story? If there was no Adam and Eve and a talking snake, why not just reject the story completely? This is a possible philosophical weakness of creationism – based on views about the strength of the argument supporting creationist beliefs.

Another possible weakness of biblical creationism lies in the challenge that there is a lack of evidence about its truth – or evidence contradicting its claims. This might focus on, for example, the difficulty of fitting two of every species harmoniously into one boat, or the lack of evidence for a flood which covered the whole world. This criticism takes the view that scientific evidence points to an alternative explanation for the origins of the universe and life on Earth and also rejects the claims of the Bible based on scientific evidence.

Talk Point

How might someone challenge the views of creationism and intelligent design – and how might a creationist respond to this?

Explanations based on creation science

Creation scientists go further than creationists and those who support intelligent design. Basically, they use scientific methods and what they consider to be evidence to support creationism. So, to support the biblical flood story, for example, they look for evidence in fossils and the geological record which they claim supports the truth of a worldwide flood. Some also argue that the age of the Earth can be scientifically shown to match the age of the Earth as described in the Bible. Their aim is to support biblical accounts of creation using scientific methods – and also to call into question alternative theories for the origin of the universe and life on Earth by challenging the scientific claims on which they are based.

Talk Point

In what different ways might scientists question the claims of creation science?

Possible strengths of explanations based on creation science

Creation scientists might argue that the key strength of their approach is that it blends faith with what they consider to be solid scientific evidence. They believe that the universe and life were created because they have two sources of evidence – faith in the biblical accounts and supporting evidence for those biblical accounts which has, in their view, scientific credibility. Some might say this means that creation scientists can engage in discussion with those who oppose divine creation of the universe and life using the same language and the same scientific levels of understanding.

Possible weaknesses of explanations based on creation science

One possible weakness of creation science might be based on views about its logic, because some feel that creation scientists start with a belief and then try to seek scientific evidence to support this belief. This is called 'confirmation bias' and many argue that this is not how science should proceed. The argument is that science should begin with a question, propose an answer and then seek to confirm or reject that answer – and the possibility of rejection is vital. The weakness could be that creation scientists do not give enough attention to any evidence which rejects their belief in divine creation (or they simply ignore it). The correct scientific approach would be to explore any possible contradictory evidence and let it speak for itself. Instead, creation scientists do not allow that their evidence might reject creation by God and that is unscientific.

Of course, many scientists reject the findings of creation scientists or their interpretations of the findings. They argue that the 'evidence' which creation science produces is not convincing and the interpretation of it is doubtful because it is based on prior belief. Any scientific finding can be interpreted in a number of ways. Creation scientists choose to interpret it in a way which is favourable to their existing viewpoint and so this calls into account their objectivity.

A second possible weakness is that creation science works on an 'if not that, then this' effect – and that this, too, is unscientific. What this means is that when the evidence does not support a particular theory (a Godless Big Bang, for example) then it must support a specific alternative (creation by God). Many argue that this is false logic because lack of evidence for one theory is not supporting evidence for an alternative theory. So even if it was proved that the Big Bang theory was completely wrong, that doesn't mean that creation must have been carried out by God.

A third possible weakness of creation science is that it can engage in argument because of the 'PhD effect', which makes it possible for some creation scientists to wrongly claim to have expertise in some areas of science. They may be well-qualified scientists, but are not well qualified in the area of science about which they are making claims. Of course, this criticism can equally apply to those who reject the claims of creation science but it should be considered when thinking about any scientific claims being made.

Explanations based on faith

Possible strengths of explanations based on faith

Talk Point

Should anyone challenge another person's beliefs?

For some, of course, the whole idea of the creation story is just far too complex – and perhaps far too remote. Many simply accept the story as a matter of faith without too much analysis of it – or perhaps none at all . This could be based on a number of factors.

Some people feel that there is no need for 'evidence' to support faith – or no real possibility of finding any. In fact, looking for such evidence is not much of an advert for your faith. Faith means believing when there's no evidence – or even where the evidence goes against your belief. In fact, perhaps those who seek scientific evidence for creation need to ask themselves why they feel the need to support their faith in this way.

Some people feel there are other 'confirmations' of belief. They argue that their religious belief – and therefore their belief in creation by God – is not based on scientific evidence of a creation (or affected by scientific evidence rejecting creation) but is based on something else: religious experience. This may be a feeling that God is there, their upbringing, their culture, social and psychological factors and so on. Faith is a complex thing, and perhaps scientific evidence and faith are just so different that there's no real 'meeting point' between the two. Perhaps science and religion should stick to what they do best.

The key strength here is that the stories are accepted on the basis of faith alone without any need for philosophical or scientific analysis.

Possible weaknesses of explanations based on faith

One possible weakness is that an approach based entirely on faith is not logical. 'Simply believing' means that any belief could be equally valid (fairies in your airing cupboard, for example). This is not a helpful way for humans to live and, in fact, could be harmful. Science has provided solutions and answers for things which used to be simply matters of belief. It does not make sense to accept scientific solutions for illness and disease (and therefore treatments) but reject scientific solutions for the creation of the universe and life. 'Simply believing' is an approach which would have kept us all in the superstitious dark ages if we had accepted it.

Another possible weakness is that the evidence rejecting the literal truth of the creation story is abundant. It makes no sense therefore to reject or ignore this evidence and doing so is potentially harmful to us as a species. If we accept that anyone or anything can be right about something just because they believe it, then our species could be in trouble. You cannot simply reject or ignore solid scientific evidence because you think it is wrong.

Religious explanations: metaphorical explanations

People accept metaphorical explanations for all sorts of reasons. Might these reasons make the claims more or less believable?

- What might motivate someone towards reaching a metaphorical understanding? Does prior belief make it more likely that you will try to explain away apparently odd or contradictory aspects of the story? Is the approach of taking a story as metaphor simply a way to avoid engaging with scientific and philosophical challenges to the truth of the story?
- How far should anyone accept someone else's metaphorical understanding? For example, should we be more inclined to accept (or reject) a metaphorical understanding if it comes from someone with 'authority' (such as a religious teacher or 'expert')?
- What's in it for the believer? What advantages does approaching the biblical creation story as metaphor give the believer compared to someone who accepts it as literally true?

So, different ways of interpreting the biblical story are based on different understandings of its nature and purpose – and probably based on a great many other things as well. Perhaps at the end of the day it is all simply a matter of belief and personal choice. Some might argue that the fact that many people still believe in the creation story in our 'scientific age' says something about its appeal for people, although others might argue that there are many reasons for its appeal. Whatever the truth of the matter – and only you can judge that – science continues to examine the evidence around the origins of the universe and life on Earth, and we will consider that in the chapters which follow.

Symbolic explanations

So if a religious person wants to believe in creation by God, but does not accept the literal truth of the biblical story, how might he or she proceed? One way is to take the view that the creation story is true, but in a symbolic way. A symbol is something which represents something else – but is not the thing itself.

Symbols convey meaning – especially where the meaning might be complex or very abstract. So, in reading the biblical creation story a number of symbols might be identified which help to understand broad aspects of the story without worrying about whether these are literally true or not. Possible symbols in the creation story include the following:

- Creation in six days represents six separate time periods where the length of time is unspecified.
- Adam and Eve represent mankind and womankind – all humans in existence at the time.
- The Garden of Eden represents a state of perfect harmony.
- The tree of knowledge represents the development of human self-awareness.
- The snake represents inner temptation of the mind.
- The flood represents an event which points towards the consequences of wickedness.

Possible strengths of symbolic explanations

Symbols might be used throughout biblical stories as a way to communicate what is otherwise too difficult to explain. This means that we understand the meaning of the story without understanding the detail. Some people have compared this to 'baby talk' – the method of adjusting your tone and the words you use when speaking to young children. Perhaps the Bible's creation story is a form of baby talk because the complexity of the creation is so great that we could not hope to understand it if it was communicated to us as it really happened.

Symbolic explanations allow religious people to accept the truth of the stories about origins without necessarily accepting everything as literally true – with all the potential issues that might raise. This also allows them to keep their faith intact, and to accept that some (or all) elements of scientific explanations can be accepted in addition to their religious views.

Possible weaknesses of symbolic explanations

One possible weakness is that this approach might imply a lack of faith. If you explain something away as a symbol rather than the literal truth, does this mean that the literal truth is too much for you to believe in and so you 'soften' it by accepting it symbolically?

What's more, where does symbolic interpretation begin and end? If you accept that some aspects of the Bible are symbolic, then why not all? If you start explaining away biblical stories, then there is a danger that you explain it all away and are left with nothing but a story. If the six days of creation are symbolic, then perhaps God is symbolic too. If you dismiss certain aspects of the Bible as symbols, then perhaps the whole Bible is just a collection of symbols.

Who decides what a symbol represents and how do we reach agreement on this (if we need to)? Is the tree of knowledge a real tree, a representative tree, a concept, an idea, an abstract suggestion? This way of understanding biblical stories might lead to a great variety of understandings and so a great variety of belief.

Another weakness of this approach is that understanding the biblical stories symbolically is just a reaction to the increasingly persuasive explanations of science. As science begins to explain more and more about our origins, the literal truth of the creation story becomes more difficult to accept – so more and more people come to understand it symbolically. Perhaps as science provides more explanation, so the Bible explains less – and so there might come a point where biblical explanations are completely replaced by scientific ones. (Some people would argue that this is already the case.)

Mythological interpretations

A myth is a story handed down through generations, sometimes by word of mouth and sometimes through the written word. Myths also contain symbols and allegories, metaphor and simile among other techniques of communication. Myths point to general truths and/or exist to explain meaning. They are generally accepted as stories which have something of a grain of truth in them, but which are expanded

Talk Point

What is a myth?

and developed to the point where it becomes hard to disentangle fact and fiction. For some, the biblical creation story is a mythological account of the events of the creation – not a literally true story, but something which points to truth.

Possible strengths of mythological interpretations

The key strength here is similar to understanding the stories as metaphor or symbolism. It allows the religious person to accept the 'big picture truth' of the story without having to explain away scientific contradictions. This means that the stories can be considered to be true, without the need for a single definition of 'true'!

Possible weaknesses of mythological interpretations

Like symbolic interpretations, understanding the biblical story as myth might be considered a weak approach because it points to a lack of faith – if faith means that you accept the story as written. Some would argue that this would be a very narrow definition of faith. However, the criticism is that in treating the story as myth, you avoid some of the difficulties associated with treating it as literally true – and perhaps through your faith you should not do so.

There are many creation myths around the world, and also many creation myths from the ancient Near East, which have great similarities to the biblical story. Why accept the biblical story and reject all the others? Basically, this is based on your belief and again is a circular argument, where you believe the biblical story to be true because your starting point is that the biblical story is true.

Similarly, treating the biblical story as myth might just be a way to avoid the challenges to the story presented by science. If you claim the story as a myth, but pointing to truth, then you do not need to respond to any scientific challenges to the truth of the creation story or any aspect of it. This can be considered a weakness but also a strength, depending on your point of view!

Personal Reflection

* *What is your response to the Bible's creation story, and how did you reach your view?*
* *What are the strengths and weaknesses of believing without evidence (or believing in the face of contradictory evidence)?*
* *How would life change if religious or scientific explanations for the origin of the universe/life on Earth were proved to be completely true?*
* *What are your views on creation stories from around the world?*
* *What questions does the Judaeo-Christian story raise for you and where might you look for answers?*
* *In your view, does the existence of the universe imply the existence of a creator?*

Apply your learning

Investigate

Find out more about:

➤ other ancient Near Eastern creation stories/myths
➤ intelligent design arguments
➤ claims and counter-claims about creation science
➤ views about creationism, intelligent design and creation science in religions other than Christianity
➤ famous public debates about creationism and creation science
➤ the *Epic of Gilgamesh*
➤ the First Cause argument
➤ evidence for and against the flood story in the Judaeo-Christian scriptures
➤ symbolic understandings of the story of Adam and Eve
➤ the extent to which different Christian groups accept the scriptural creation story as literally true
➤ creation science and intelligent design.

For each of these, report your findings in a manner of your choice. This could be a written report or presentation — in the form of tables, graphs and charts — or as the source of material for a class debate or discussion. You should select a method for your report which is most appropriate for the aspect you are investigating.

Active Learning

1 Re-tell one creation story (not the Judaeo-Christian story) from around the world in a format of your choice. This could be art, music, drama or a combination of the three. Now do the same for the Judaeo-Christian story. You should consider in some depth any questions which might be raised about each aspect of the story. Think of a way to identify these questions in your re-telling of the story (such as speech bubbles on a piece of artwork) and use the questions as the basis for a discussion.

2 Create a question wall for your classroom where you write up as many questions about creation stories as you can in one colour and as many answers to the questions as you can in another colour.

3 In the format of a TV chat show, script an interview about the Judaeo-Christian creation story with three guests: one who thinks it is literally true, one who thinks it is metaphorically true and one who thinks it is not true at all.

4 Imagine you have been invited to your local primary school. The Primary 3 class is learning about the story of Noah. Your task is to help them to ask questions about the story and to think through the answers which might be given by a range of people, religious and non-religious.

5 Produce a piece of writing using one of the following statements as your title. Ideally you should choose a title you *do not* agree with.
   ➤ 'The existence of the universe suggests there is a God.'
   ➤ 'There is no need for a creator of the universe.'

6 Script a dialogue between three religious people: one who accepts the creation story as literally true, one who thinks it is metaphor and one who thinks it is mythology. If you like, you could write the script in a Scots dialect.

7 Create your own artwork of the biblical creation story and annotate it with explanations of possible symbols in the story.

8   There has been a lot of debate in Scotland about how far creationism and creation science should be studied in school. The current view taken by the government is that it can be studied in RMPS but not in science. There is also a view that teachers should not express their own views about creationism or creation science. Have a class discussion about this – bearing in mind that it is a sensitive topic for some.

9   In the *Investigate* tasks, you may have investigated further myths such as the *Epic of Gilgamesh*. Create a table of similarities and differences between this (and any other similar creation myths) and the biblical creation story. Do the similarities/differences support and/or question the truth of any of the stories?

10 A child (you decide what age) in a religious family one day asks their parents this question: 'Did God really make everything like the Bible says he did?' Write the answer you think the parents might give.

Check Your Understanding

1   What creation stories are there around the world?

2   Describe one possible question raised by the existence of many creation stories around the world.

3   Describe one possible response to the variety of creation stories around the world.

4   In your own words, describe the Judaeo-Christian version of the creation of the universe.

5   Describe the creation of human beings according to Genesis.

6   What questions might be raised about the disobedience of Adam and Eve and the story of Noah?

7   What might be the origins of the Judaeo-Christian creation story?

8   Describe two possible responses to the potential 'truth' of the Genesis creation story and offer your own views on these.

9   Describe two things the creation story might tell us about the nature of a creator.

10 In what ways might the universe and life in it point to a good creator or some other kind of being?

11 What issues are raised by the First Cause argument for religious and non-religious people?

12 What evidence do religious people use for the existence of a creator and how might non-religious people respond to this?

13 Why might many religious people think it is perfectly reasonable to believe in a creator?

14 What might human nature tell us about the nature of a creator?

15 Describe two different meanings of biblical creationism.

16 Explain two possible weaknesses of biblical creationism.

17 Describe two differences between creationism and creation science.

18 Describe two possible strengths of creation science.

19 How might 'confirmation bias' play a part in understanding the biblical creation story?

20 What is meant by interpreting the creation story as symbolic?

21 Describe two possible symbols in the biblical creation story.

22 Explain one possible weakness of a symbolic understanding of the creation story.

23 Is understanding the biblical creation story as myth different from understanding it as symbolic? Explain your answer.

24 How might the existence of other creation myths affect the truth of the biblical creation story?

25 In what ways might literary genres in the Bible influence our understanding of biblical accounts of creation?

26 What role does (or should) faith play in understanding the creation story?

27 In what ways might religious people defend their belief in the creation story?

Analyse and Evaluate

1 'Religious people and non-religious people will never agree about the existence of a creator.' Discuss.

2 'If one creation story is true, this makes all the others false.' Discuss this statement.

3 'You don't need evidence to dismiss the existence of a creator; reason is enough.' Discuss this claim.

4 To what extent does a Jewish/Christian person have to accept the scriptural creation story as literally true?

5 'Since religion is about faith — all that is needed to believe in a creator is faith.' How far do religious and non-religious people agree with this statement?

6 'There is no real point in thinking about whether the universe was created or not.' Discuss.

7 In what ways are creationism, intelligent design and creation science similar and different?

8 'It is reasonable to believe in the literal truth of the biblical creation story.' Discuss.

9 'You can understand the biblical creation story as metaphor but still take it to be true.' Discuss.

10 Analyse the view that a non-literal interpretation of the biblical creation story suggests a lack of faith.

11 To what extent should religious people accept the claims of creation science?

Scientific explanations and evidence

3

Two elderly 'ladies who lunch' meet up for their usual Monday high tea in a small tea shop in the Morningside area of Edinburgh. As ever, following the usual pleasantries about the weather and the mysterious goings-on at Number 24, they turn their attention to the deeper questions of life ...

Karen: I watched this television programme about the Big Bang last night and my head still hurts ...

Sharon: I can imagine, that's why I stick to the radio dramas, my dear — easy on the grey cells. *The Archers* is much less taxing at our age.

Karen: Yes, you are correct, of course, but occasionally I like to stretch my thinking somewhat — a pleasant change from the daffodil tea-mornings and the idle chatter of Daphne and her tiresome circle of acolytes.

Sharon: Indeed, Daphne is quite wearing isn't she, and those frocks ...

Karen: Quite so. Anyway, they were saying that everything in the universe began with a Big Bang — and there was a time when there was no time ... And there was nowhere either.

Sharon: So when and where did this Big Bang happen?

Karen: Well, there wasn't a when, the when only happened after the Big Bang.

Sharon: If there was an after, there must have been a before.

Karen: No, there wasn't and there also wasn't an anywhere.

Sharon: But if the Big Bang happened, and from some point it was somewhere when before it hadn't been somewhere, then before it would need to have been nowhere, but nowhere is still in some way somewhere, isn't it?

→

Karen: The scientists say not, dear. 'Where' the Big Bang happened is everywhere there is now – right at this doily-covered tea table, in fact.

Sharon: So the Big Bang happened here – in this cosy little tea shop in Edinburgh?

Karen: I suppose that must be what they mean – absolutely – here, on Morningside Road.

Sharon: Well, that's certainly something to be thinking about, isn't it? I imagine that if it means everywhere now, then the Big Bang also happened inside this cup of Earl Grey … and in that delicate little fairy cake on the top plate.

Karen: I suppose that is what it must mean – though I would be the first to admit that I could in no way be considered scientific.

Sharon: Nor I, my dear. Now if this Big Bang caused time, then what happened before this Big Bang?

Karen: Nothing, I imagine – for time hadn't been invented yet.

Sharon: I can see why anyone might come over all giddy about this. The only solution as far as I can see is that rather delicious-looking chocolate eclair, don't you think?

Karen: Oh, yes, indeed – there's no question in the universe that can't be answered by a chocolate eclair …

Talk Point

How do you think the universe began?

What is the Big Bang?

There are competing scientific theories about the origins of the universe, including Steady State theory, Big Bounce theory, Eternal Inflation theory, Oscillating Universe theory and probably some others which may or may not be scientific. However, for the purposes of this course we will work on the basis that the Big Bang theory is currently the most widely accepted within the scientific community. You should note that this is sometimes referred to as the standard model of Big Bang theory – since other models are available. Recently, some theoretical physicists have been asking questions about the Big Bang theory based on quantum theory – and suggesting that perhaps the universe did not, in fact, have a beginning, but has always existed. The physics is very complex but it is important to keep up to date, because between the writing of this book and your exam, scientists might just have come up with a different theory which replaces (the standard model of) Big Bang theory: you have been warned.

The current view held by scientists is that the universe began with what has come to be known as the Big Bang. It would be easy to think of this as an explosion or expansion 'out' into something, but it's not – it was an expansion of itself, and it is still expanding today. This point of initial expansion is known as a singularity and this initial singularity came into being 13.8 billion years or so ago. Physicists would love to know exactly what this initial singularity was like but at the moment they don't (and some are not sure about the singularity idea at all). What they think is that all matter, space and time were 'contained within' this singularity which, for a reason as yet unknown (though linked to the laws of physics), began a rapid expansion to become everything that we know today. This includes you, by the way.

Physicists think that the singularity was a 'beginning', in that space, time and matter all began at the moment of the initial singularity's rapid expansion. What prompted this change of state is not currently known, but scientists generally take the view that any cause will have been due to the neutral laws of physics and not a causal agent of any kind.

It is important to make a distinction between the origins of the universe and the origins of the Earth. The Big Bang theory centres on the singularity and so the beginning of space, time and matter. Once matter began this expansion, gravitational and other forces in physics pulled matter together to form galaxies, stars, planets, moons and all other astronomical bodies. The Earth is an accretion of matter which came together to form a small planet.

Scientific evidence

Evidence in science can take one of two formats:

▸ **Empirical evidence** This is evidence from observation and experiment and involves drawing conclusions from observable reality.
▸ **Theoretical evidence** This is evidence which might have its starting point in empirical evidence, or may begin instead as a theory awaiting the possibility of gathering empirical evidence when it is possible to do so. (For example, when suitable measuring technology is designed.)

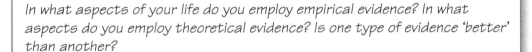

Talk Point

In what aspects of your life do you employ empirical evidence? In what aspects do you employ theoretical evidence? Is one type of evidence 'better' than another?

In science, sometimes the evidence comes first through observation and experiment (and sometimes the evidence comes in unexpected ways). When this happens, the theory builds around the evidence while all the time seeking out challenges to this evidence and better understandings of this evidence. It is crucial in science that any conflicting evidence is treated very seriously, since this might provide a better theory or solution.

Other times the theory comes first and the evidence later. What this does not mean is that scientists go looking for evidence to support their theory. (And they would not ignore any evidence which contradicted their theory.) What it does mean is that scientists note evidence which supports or rejects their theory and give an equal level of importance to all the evidence – no matter what it points to.

In general, no matter what the evidence is, a scientific theory must be able to pass two important 'tests':

▸ It must be verifiable, that is capable of being shown to be true through evidence.
▸ It must be falsifiable, that is capable of being shown to be false through evidence. Science is, in fact, based on the idea of the 'latest and best fit' for the available evidence – and scientists pride themselves on their willingness to be shown to be wrong. In fact, showing one thing to be wrong and replacing it with something better is actually how science makes progress.

Scientific evidence for the Big Bang

There are three main sources of empirical evidence for the Big Bang: cosmic background radiation, redshift of light due to an expanding universe and the relative abundance of the elements.

Cosmic background radiation

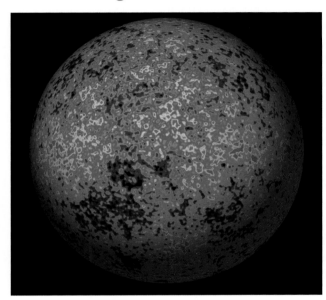

When the universe began there was an unimaginable amount of heat around. This heat was in the electromagnetic spectrum or, more specifically, microwave energy. As the universe expands, this microwave energy can still be detected today – and is often referred to as cosmic background radiation (CBR). CBR has specific temperature ranges and, as measured today, suggests that the universe began as the Big Bang theory claims it did.

Interestingly, the existence of CBR itself throws up some problems. For example, some physicists argue that CBR should be distributed evenly throughout the universe but it is not and there is disagreement about why this is the case. Its temperature shows variation across the universe and there are 'clumps' of higher and lower temperatures. In fact, there seems to be a 'preferred' direction of temperature variation and an interesting big area (or 'cold spot') where there's nothing much of anything. Some physicists wonder if this points to universes beyond our own.

Redshift of light due to an expanding universe

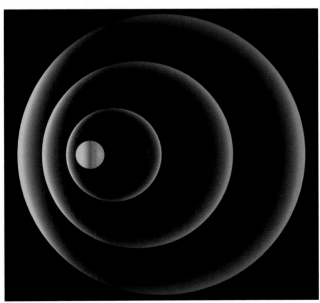

The spectrum of light coming from the galaxies in the universe seems to shift towards the red end of the light spectrum. This means that the observed light's wavelength appears longer. This is what you would expect to see when objects in the universe are moving away from us and from each other – as would happen as a result of the Big Bang as the universe expands. This is what we observe, therefore it supports Big Bang theory. Additionally, the relatively recent discovery of direct evidence of gravitational waves (not to be confused with gravity waves), as predicted theoretically by Einstein, is considered by most scientists to be further proof that the universe expanded very quickly just as the Big Bang theory claims.

Relative abundance of the elements

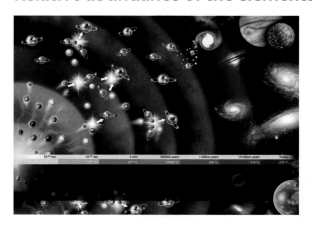

Big Bang theory proposes that all the matter in the universe was formed by the process of 'Big Bang nucleosynthesis' and that the chemical elements we know of today were all formed as the universe expanded and cooled. The theory also suggests how much of each element would have been made, and when scientists look at old stars and distant galaxies they see the proportions of hydrogen, helium and other trace elements as predicted by the theory. This evidence points to the likelihood that the universe began according to Big Bang theory.

For scientists, these three observable, measurable and verifiable pieces of evidence show that the universe began according to Big Bang theory.

The Big Bang theory

Possible strengths of Big Bang theory

First, scientists would argue that the key strength of Big Bang theory is that it is evidence-based, not based on simple beliefs or on the authority of some scripture or alleged divine revelation. The evidence for Big Bang theory given above is repeatedly agreed across the scientific community, which scientists would argue increases its reliability and validity and so makes it extremely likely to be true. The vast majority of scientists accept the Big Bang theory of the origins of the universe because they accept the evidence available as indicating that the Big Bang happened as the theory states. The evidence can be verified and it can be measured and quantified. It supports the theory, therefore the theory is true.

However, some would argue that, in fact, scientists give only qualified acceptance to any theory (and there is often discussion in science about when a theory becomes a fact). Science works on the principle of the best fit between the current evidence and current theories. Again, for the vast majority of scientists, the current evidence best fits the standard Big Bang model of the origins of the universe and so this is the theory which best explains the origins of the universe. However, scientists will continue to question and challenge the Big Bang theory (as with all scientific theories), to propose new theories and to interpret the evidence available. Also, scientists discover new evidence about things all the time – so there may yet be new evidence which confirms or calls into question the Big Bang theory. That's how science works and scientists are confident that this process of evidence being open to challenge, questioning and, if necessary, rejection and amendment, is one of its key strengths.

Possible weaknesses of Big Bang theory

There are some scientists who think there are weaknesses in Big Bang theory. These weaknesses may include their belief that the evidence has been misinterpreted, or simply does not point to what the majority of scientists think it points to, or that some alternative theory is a better explanation for the available evidence. There are some, too, who might argue that the absence of conclusive evidence about aspects of the Big Bang calls into question the theory, though most would respond to this by saying 'absence of evidence is not evidence of absence' – the evidence is the best we have and provides the best explanation. It is important to remember that science welcomes such challenges, provided they are based on evidence, because continued questioning and searching for evidence might uncover something new and relevant. However, the scientific community would be unlikely to accept a scientist who rejects the evidence based on his or her beliefs (in the absence of scientific evidence).

Another possible weakness of Big Bang theory is based less on scientific evidence than on philosophical grounds – no matter what the evidence says. For example, it could be argued that it is philosophically meaningless to talk about a 'time' when there was no time, or 'somewhere' which could not exist since nowhere existed. Such things might be regarded as as logical impossibilities – and something logically impossible may also be actually impossible. Because of this, someone could reject the apparent evidence because it is not logically possible for the universe to have begun as Big Bang theory claims it did.

A further possible weakness of Big Bang theory is likely to come from a specifically religious perspective. Some people simply dismiss Big Bang theory because it does not require the creative action of a God (and it possibly contradicts scriptural accounts of the origins of the universe). The Big Bang theory proposes that the universe needed no external cause – rather, it caused itself. This would remove the need for a creator, and for some religious people that suggestion is unacceptable. Scientists would, of course, respond that something being philosophically unacceptable does not make it untrue. However, it is important to point out that many religious people accept the Big Bang theory of the origins of the universe because while it proposes no need for a creator, it does not provide evidence for the absence of a creator. This means that religious people can accept Big Bang theory but also believe that a creator God was involved as well. This means that scientists can also be religious people.

We will return to the question of how far you can accept the Big Bang theory and creation by God in the final chapter in this topic.

I hope you're sitting comfortably because I'm going to tell you a story. It's a story about a little fluffy wasp named Agnes and a slinky caterpillar named Charlie. This is probably not a story you'll want to pass on to your little brother or sister, not if you don't want to be kept awake all night by their screams …

Agnes the wasp spends most of her days buzzing around, feeding and enjoying the lovely summer days. She knows she's a wasp and that some people don't like wasps, but she prides herself on being quite a nice wasp. She spends each day flitting from leaf to leaf, tree to tree and generally flying around having a lovely time, soaking up the toasty sunshine.

Eventually, as happens to wasps, Agnes realises that it is time to have some baby wasps. Now Agnes does the strangest thing. She sees Charlie the caterpillar most days. Charlie is long and green and wiggly, and spends most of his day chomping through great big squishy green leaves – moving slowly up and down the branches. He doesn't mind that he looks a bit comical, for one day, he's been told, he will become the most beautiful butterfly – or, as it is about to turn out, perhaps not. When Agnes is ready to lay her eggs she finds poor old Charlie munching away as ever and, rather oddly – and a matter of great surprise to Charlie – she injects her eggs into Charlie. This nips a bit and Charlie is rather offended by this quite inappropriate action towards him by Agnes. Unfortunately, Charlie is not really aware that Agnes has deposited her eggs inside his body and he cheerily carries on as normal. Before long he has something of a tummy upset – perhaps he ate too many leaves in one day, he thinks. But this tummy upset becomes something quite different and really rather uncomfortable, in fact.

To cut a long story short, Charlie really begins to feel not very well at all. It's hard to say if he is in any pain or not – after all, he's a caterpillar, and caterpillars are not generally the kind of creatures to talk about their feelings, though perhaps Charlie just needs to let it all out a bit more. Sadly, what Charlie does not know is that the eggs which Agnes has laid inside his body have hatched into little wasp larvae who now start to feed on the unfortunate Charlie … from the inside out. Eventually, poor old Charlie is no more and the cheeky little wasp larvae emerge from his now lifeless dried-up body as tiny little baby wasps who live happily ever after. Charlie, of course, doesn't …

Note: to protect their identities 'Charlie' and 'Agnes' are not their real names.

What is evolution?

Evolution can be summed up as follows:

▶ There are various mechanisms for reproduction
▶ When living things reproduce, the offspring are not carbon-copies of the parent but different
▶ Sometimes this difference is caused by a random genetic mutation
▶ Such mutations might not provide any benefit to the organism – if so, they're likely to die out
▶ However, when a mutation provides an advantage to an organism in a particular context, it is far more likely to survive
▶ The advantageous mutation is therefore more likely to be passed on to subsequent offspring
▶ Over time, this 'natural selection' can lead to very small changes adding up even to the point of creating new species.

Talk Point

What does the above sad little tale suggest about the reality of nature?

Evolution or evolutionary theory?

Some species of parasitic wasps have indeed developed to lay their eggs inside living hosts, for these eggs to hatch and the developing young to eat their way out, killing the host organism in the process. According to evolutionary theory, these wasps have developed – or evolved – this behaviour to ensure their continued survival over millions of years. As yet, some of their hosts have not evolved to avoid this rather unpleasant experience – so they have some catching up to do. So what is evolution?

Some argue that evolution is not a theory – it is a fact, and so we should not refer to 'evolutionary theory' but simply to 'evolution'. In science, an observation becomes a fact when it has been repeatedly confirmed and has not been rejected. However, science works on the principle of the best explanation using the best available evidence – so what is considered to be fact is the best explanation available to us now using the evidence available to us at the present time. This means, of course, that what is considered to be a fact today might no longer be a fact tomorrow if new evidence is discovered and/or new and better explanations are provided for the evidence currently available. So, in principle, evolution could be challenged tomorrow by the discovery of new evidence or a change in thinking about the evidence we have – and could then be discarded and replaced with a new explanation for the origin and development of life on Earth. Many scientists point out that this has not happened since Charles Darwin (1809–1882) first proposed his theory of evolution and, in fact, further evidence has been uncovered to support the theory, therefore evolution is the best scientific explanation we have for the origin and development of life on Earth … and therefore it is a fact. The discussion is ongoing. Remember that in science, something must, in principle, be verifiable and falsifiable, and that theories can develop from observations or the theories can come first and patiently await available evidence.

Charles Darwin.

Scientific evidence for evolution

As far as evolution is concerned, Charles Darwin made observations and uncovered evidence which did not fit with the accepted view about the origins and development of life on Earth at the time of his work. In Darwin's day, the creation of life on Earth was generally accepted to be as the Bible described it – quite literally. Darwin began to uncover evidence that called into question the literal truth of the biblical account of creation. As he uncovered more and more evidence, he built up a theory to explain this evidence. However, Darwin himself was so troubled by his findings and his emerging evolutionary theory that he kept it under close wraps for a long time. There are conflicting views about Darwin's own religious beliefs throughout his life but his wife, Emma Wedgwood, was a devout Christian, and he worried about the possible outcomes for other people's religious beliefs if his theory was made public. These two facts probably explain his reluctance to publish his findings for quite some time.

So what was the evidence which troubled Darwin so much?

The geological record

Darwin, like many people in his day, was fascinated by the natural world and its many aspects. He was a keen geologist and it is perhaps in this area that he first began to question the biblical creation story. According to the Bible, the Earth's age can be numbered in thousands of years, but the evidence in the geological record suggested that the Earth was much older – in fact, findings by Charles Lyall suggested that the geological record showed the Earth to be many millions of years old. In addition to this, the geological record did not show any evidence of a global flood as described in the Bible. Clearly, this evidence challenged the biblical account of creation. If the geological record threw doubt upon the biblical creation story, might there be other evidence out there which might also challenge creation as the origin of life on Earth?

The fossil record

Perhaps even more troubling for Darwin was the fossil record – the record of fossilised life forms throughout geological time. This suggested two important things. First, there was evidence of the extinction of whole species throughout time – there were fossils of creatures which no longer existed and had not done so for a very long time. What could explain God creating whole species of life and then simply getting rid of them, for them never to return? As well as this, there was evidence of development of life throughout time – with organisms becoming more and more complex as time went on. Some living organisms shared features with fossilised ones – although there were differences too. However, the similarities often raised questions about how unique each species might be. None of this matched the biblical account which claimed that everything was made in the beginning exactly as it remains today. In addition to this, there was evidence to suggest that humans arrived on the scene quite late on in the Earth's history and that they did not live side by side with some creatures (such as the dinosaurs) that were extinct long before humans arrived. Perhaps more concerning, there was evidence that there were other forms of humans on Earth before humans as we know them today. This further called into question the belief that humans were made in the beginning exactly as they appear today, that all life was created at a fixed point in time and that life forms on Earth today are exactly as they had been throughout Earth's history.

Talk Point

In what ways might the fossil record challenge belief in creation by a divine being?

Geographical specificity of life

Some argue that Darwin's famous voyage on HMS *Beagle* from 1831 to 1836 finally confirmed his growing theory about how life originated and developed on Earth. On this trip – which involved many varied ports of call – Darwin began to notice that different species seemed to be specifically located in certain parts of the world, and there alone. If all life had been created by God 'in the beginning', then why did he create certain species to live only in certain places? Darwin's visit to the remote and isolated Galápagos Islands created more questions. Here, on one small island, there were small finches with quite big, strong beaks; on another island not that far away, there were similar finches, but here their beaks were fine

and delicate. Why would God populate one island with only big-beaked finches and another with only fine-beaked ones? Interestingly, Darwin noticed that the foods these birds ate matched perfectly their beak type. Of course, this could have meant that God created a certain beak to match a certain food type. Alternatively, and this is how Darwin began to think more and more, perhaps the food type led to the development of a certain type of finch. Darwin began to talk about the 'transmutation of species' and the first glimmers of evidence for evolution by natural selection were beginning to appear.

Breeding programmes

Darwin knew well that farmers and, interestingly, pigeon-breeders, could breed selectively from certain animals to produce desirable characteristics. In fact, he engaged in some pigeon-breeding experiments himself and discovered that specific qualities in a pigeon could be produced by selectively breeding repeated offspring until you had your desired outcome. For example, let's say that there is a ratio between wingspan and body size which seems to lead to pigeons which are very successful racers. Starting with an ordinary pigeon, you breed offspring from this pigeon. You then breed again from this offspring but you only breed from those who have something a little closer to the body:wingspan ratio you are looking for. You then breed again from their offspring, and from theirs and theirs and so on. Each time you select for further breeding only those offspring who show something like the desired body:wingspan ratio you're looking for. Eventually, after many generations, you have what you're looking for – a pigeon with the perfect body:wingspan ratio to win races. This process was well known to breeders even in Darwin's day and is known as 'artificial selection'.

Now this was the key point for Darwin – could it be that a similar process happened in nature, and that nature itself selected successive offspring to survive provided they matched 'desirable' criteria? How would these criteria themselves come about? Darwin's solution was simple. The criterion for breeding in nature is the environment in which an organism lives. If successive offspring are better suited to the environment in which they live, they go on to survive, breed and increase in number. So this would mean that nature was selecting which offspring would survive and continue. Darwin called this 'evolution by natural selection'. This explained his Galápagos finches. There would have been finches with both kinds of beaks in the first instance but if the food source on one island was large tough nuts, then the finches who – by chance – had the biggest and strongest beaks would be more likely to be able to eat, survive and reproduce, especially compared to their fine-beaked friends. Eventually, this environmental condition would lead to a population composed only of big-beaked birds and there would be no fine beaks anywhere to be seen (except on the next island where the food source was more suitable for fine-beaked birds).

Similarities across species – anatomy and behaviour

So Darwin had the mechanism for this process of natural selection – and now he began to gather further evidence. For example, he noticed that many organisms share a basic shape or basic organs and structures – in fact, the embryos of many different species look remarkably similar at their early stages of development. Why would this be? One possibility is that many different species developed from common ancestors and, at one point, these ancestral lines branched away from each other. This would explain why hearts and lungs and arms and legs and mouths and so on, are all relatively similar across some very different species. Darwin was also very interested in behaviour (some people consider him to be the first real psychologist). He noted that certain behaviours and emotions in the animal world – such as fear, anger and sadness – seemed very similar across many different species, including humans. Could this mean that these species all shared a common origin? Could it be that human behaviours and emotions were not all that different from those of other animals? If so, this suggested a much closer relationship between humans and other animals than many at the time (and even today) would have been happy to accept, and it called into serious question the view that humans are unique creatures and the peak of creation.

Talk Point

Why might so many creatures share so many features?

Vestigial features

Darwin began to add to his theory a question about vestigial features across species. Vestigial features are bodily structures which seem to have no purpose. Take the appendix in humans, for example. This seems to serve no purpose in our body (except sometimes to cause us problems) and yet other species have a much larger appendix, where it seems to have the function of storing helpful bacteria which help to break down certain foodstuffs. Since humans do not (or no longer) eat such foodstuffs, perhaps our once larger and useful appendix has, over successive generations, become smaller and useless. This might point to closer relationships between species (including humans) and some common ancestry, which was a horrifying thought for many in Darwin's day. It questioned both any basic design which a creator God might have used, and the uniqueness of different species.

The struggle for survival

Through the evidence of past extinctions and the complex relationship between food supply and population levels, Darwin also began to question creation by God as the way in which life began and developed. Past extinctions seemed very closely linked to catastrophic events. Since God was all-powerful and perfectly good, why did he allow such events to lead to the complete extinction of many living things? Darwin argued that life itself was a struggle for survival, with only those best suited to a particular environment being likely to survive and produce offspring. His own family circumstances sadly supported this – and probably became a great source of torment for him. His wife was actually quite closely related to him (this was very common at the time) and his children suffered from many illnesses and three of them died at a young age. Darwin was tortured by the possibility that this was evolution in action – the closeness of his family relationship with his wife weakened their offspring. At the time, no one knew the mechanisms of genetics but it was known that the closer the family relationship between a breeding pair (including humans), the more likelihood there was of negative consequences for the offspring.

Darwin must have questioned this repeatedly. If life was a struggle for survival where only those best suited to a specific environment lived, what did this say about the nature of any creator? Perhaps Darwin's decision not to publish his theory *On the Origin of Species by Means of Natural Selection* until 1859, 23 years after the return from his worldwide tour on HMS *Beagle*, was partly due to this interpretation of life as a struggle for survival.

The mechanisms of evolution

Mutation leading to adaptation

All life on Earth exists in a specific environment – whether this is a particularly narrow environment such as extremes of heat or cold, or just the global environment where certain conditions apply everywhere. The organisms most likely to survive in any environment are those which are best suited to that environment. For example, if you live in an extremely hot place then you need to have a good cooling mechanism, or be smart enough to avoid the hottest parts of the day. If you haven't got these adaptations you won't last long and you will not produce offspring. In order to survive and reproduce, an organism needs to be suited to its environmental conditions. If those environmental conditions change, then the organism needs to be able to adapt accordingly. This may take many generations, of course, but if the organism cannot adapt, then it will eventually be replaced with one which can – and this organism's offspring will survive and prosper.

These adaptations might take many millions of years and work through a series of increasingly useful steps. The development of the eye is often used as an example. In evolution, 'eyes' probably began as a few light-sensitive cells in an organism which enabled it to distinguish movement, perhaps, or light and dark areas. This might have enabled it to avoid being eaten (when its fellow organisms without the light-sensitive cells could not) and so be more likely to pass on this successful adaptation to its offspring. Over millions of years, these specialised light-sensitive cells increased in number and complexity – resulting in eyes which can distinguish movement, colour, pattern and everything else that eyes can do. Let's imagine that in years to come aliens who enjoy eating people arrive on Earth, but they can only be seen in the infrared part of the electromagnetic spectrum. Perhaps some mutation will lead to the birth of a human who can 'see' in the infrared part of the spectrum. That person will have a great evolutionary advantage and be more likely to produce successful offspring compared to those of us without the infrared sight ability.

The causes and effects of mutations

Now the interesting question which Darwin couldn't answer in his day was how these mutations came about in the first place. The answer was discovered in the twentieth century in the form of DNA. DNA is essentially the code for a living thing – the instruction book, if you like. It is formed of base pairs of nucleic acids which 'code for' specific things (in very complex ways that we don't always fully understand, even today). The DNA of both reproductive partners combine to produce DNA which is unique to each of their offspring. Every now and again – for reasons unknown – DNA mutates, or changes slightly, and this leads to changes in the developing organism. If those changes give an advantage in a particular environment (perhaps alien-seeing, infrared-receiving light cells in your eyes – or somewhere else, for that matter), then they confer evolutionary advantage – and so increase the likelihood of surviving and passing on those advantageous bits of DNA to the lucky offspring.

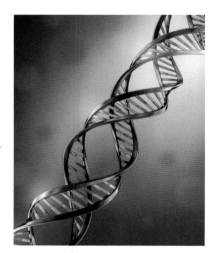

Unanswered questions about evolution

The vast majority of scientists accept evolution as the explanation for the *development* of life on Earth. However, there remains an unanswered question about the *origin* of life on Earth. What remains unclear is how inorganic matter combined and developed to become organic matter. Some scientists argue that this is not as big a problem as it might seem, and cite some interesting experiments which have simulated the likely conditions on the early Earth. These experiments have produced some evidence of early building blocks of life in the form of amino acids being able to be made from inorganic sources. Of course, scientists don't know exactly what the early conditions were like on Earth and a simulation is not the same as the real thing. So, while theories propose that organic somehow developed from inorganic, this is something which has still to be scientifically demonstrated beyond all doubt.

Other unanswered questions relate to where there are gaps in the evidence for evolution. For example, in many places there is nothing to show how one species led to another. However, for scientists, any gaps are there to be filled and do not mean that the theory is wrong, just that it is incomplete at this point. They might also add that there is no particular need to fill any of the gaps in the evidence with the actions of a divine creator.

Possible strengths of evolution theory

Most scientists accept evolution unquestioningly. In their view, the evidence is both sound and convincing, and far more credible than any alternative possibility. Like Big Bang theory, evolution is based on firm scientific evidence and on reasonable deduction where the evidence is inconclusive and/or not yet present. For scientists, this is the best way to make sense of the origin and development of life on earth. They believe it is the best-fit explanation for the evidence we currently have.

Many scientists take the view that evolutionary theory still has some 'gaps' in the evidence, such as 'missing links' in relation to fossil evidence. Again, like all science, accepting something as true always comes with an element of doubt – which is what leads to progress in science. Scientists will continue to gather evidence about all manner of things – and if this evidence continues to support or begins to challenge evolution, then so be it. The evidence for evolution matches the need for something to be, in principle, verifiable and falsifiable and, of course, science takes the view that evolution is both theoretically the best fit for the available evidence and able to draw upon observable evidence.

There was a competing theory to evolution back in Darwin's day, in the form of Lamarckian evolution (named after the French biologist Jean-Baptiste Lamarck (1744–1829)). This only really differed from evolution by natural selection in its proposal that individuals and species could adapt to environmental changes during their lifetime, and pass on these adaptations to their offspring. It would be hard to find any scientists today who would support Lamarckian evolution. Similarly, it is difficult to find any scientifically accepted alternative to evolution (apart from those linked to religious belief, but more of that in the next chapter). That's not to say that scientists do not continue to interpret evidence linked to evolution and ask themselves how far it supports or rejects evolution, but that's what scientists do. So far, the mainstream scientific community has yet to give credibility to any potential alternative theory – but remember, things change in science, so who knows?

Possible weaknesses of evolution theory

As well as potential scientific challenges to evolution theory, some might question the evidence for evolution because they consider there is something unique about human life which sets it apart from other living things. They might call this difference a soul or consciousness or self-awareness or whatever, but their argument is that philosophically speaking, humans are different from other forms of life on Earth in such important ways that it calls into question the development of humans from other life forms. Science is, of course, making headway in understanding consciousness but there is no scientific way of providing evidence for the existence of anything resembling a 'soul' in humans. Likewise, there is no evidence for or against the existence of any kind of 'soul' in any other life form.

One final possible weakness of scientific explanations of the origin of life is not exclusively linked to evolutionary theory but to the initial circumstances in which life originated. The scientific argument is that organic life spontaneously developed from inorganic life through a process which is currently not known. Some have suggested that accepting this change (which they would argue is a pretty major one) from inorganic to organic is a weakness of scientific explanations because any possible evidence for the mechanism which allowed it to happen has yet to be uncovered.

Personal Reflection

* What would be the consequences if the Big Bang was proved beyond any possible doubt to be how the universe began?
* What are your views on Big Bang theory — and, just as importantly, where did your views about Big Bang theory come from?
* Science does not accept anything without evidence. In your view, what counts and what doesn't count as evidence?
* How important do you think it is for humans to understand how life on Earth began and developed?
* What is your response to the evidence supporting evolution outlined in this chapter?
* In what ways do you think evolution might challenge religious belief?

Apply your learning

Active Learning

1. In a group, devise a list of questions — about anything, anywhere, any time. (For example, 'Is the planet furthest away from planet Earth made of toffee?') Now pass these questions to another group who will categorise them as follows: verifiable in principle; falsifiable in principle; unverifiable; unfalsifiable.
2. Using the lists of questions you have from the first activity, add a comment to each question to indicate whether you think it can best be answered using empirical or theoretical evidence — or a combination of both. Explain your choices.
3. Create your own infographic about Big Bang theory, explaining what it is, the evidence for it and the various challenges which the theory faces.
4. Prepare a series of interview questions (and conduct the interviews, if possible) for four people: a scientist who is not religious and accepts the Big Bang, a scientist who is religious and accepts the Big Bang, a religious person (who is not a scientist) who accepts the Big Bang and a religious person (who is not a scientist) who does not accept the Big Bang. Once you have your questions you could nominate people in your class to perform each role and ask them the questions.
5. Write up a journal for Darwin where he outlines his thoughts about his emerging theory of evolution by natural selection. You could choose a specific time period for this, or link it to his voyage on HMS *Beagle* or to a particular time in his life.
6. Get hold of a copy of the original text of *On the Origin of Species by Means of Natural Selection*. Select a few passages from the text which tell the story of evolution. Create a display of these passages (perhaps you could illustrate them) and add your own explanatory comments.
7. Create a presentation on evolution in a format of your choice where you outline the evidence and any challenges to it.
8. In groups, consider possible environmental futures on Earth and how these might affect which species survive and which do not. (For example, a 50 per cent reduction in the amount of sunlight reaching the Earth.) Once your group has chosen a possible environmental future, you should share it with another group who will consider the implications of it for developing life on Earth.

Investigate

Find out more about:

- ➤ the detailed scientific evidence for Big Bang theory and how it came to be formed as a theory
- ➤ some of the questions scientists still have about Big Bang theory
- ➤ scientific alternatives to the Big Bang
- ➤ philosophical questions about Big Bang theory
- ➤ religious responses to Big Bang theory across a range of religions
- ➤ physicists and cosmologists who are also religious people
- ➤ famous public debates about Big Bang theory and creation by God
- ➤ Darwin's life, his beliefs, how he handled his developing theory and responses to the theory in his day
- ➤ the geological and fossil record supporting evolution and challenges to these records
- ➤ evidence for convergent and divergent evolution
- ➤ how DNA links to genetic mutation
- ➤ scientific and non-scientific (not religious) alternatives to evolution.

For each of these, report your findings in a manner of your choice. This could be a written report or presentation – in the form of tables, graphs and charts – or as the source of material for a class debate or discussion. You should select a method for your report which is most appropriate for the aspect you are investigating.

Check Your Understanding

1 Name two scientific theories which are alternatives to the Big Bang.
2 Why might some argue that the use of the word 'explosion' is not accurate in relation to the Big Bang?
3 Describe the main features of Big Bang theory.
4 What is the difference between empirical and theoretical evidence in science?
5 Explain what is meant by 'verifiable' and 'falsifiable' in science.
6 How does the existence of cosmic background radiation support Big Bang theory?
7 What is redshift and how does it support Big Bang theory?
8 In what ways does the relative abundance of the elements in the universe support Big Bang theory?
9 Describe one challenge to one of the three major pieces of evidence of Big Bang theory.
10 What does it mean to say that some scientists accept the Big Bang theory in a 'qualified' way?
11 How might someone reject Big Bang theory on philosophical grounds?
12 Why might a religious person reject Big Bang theory?
13 Could a religious person accept Big Bang theory?
14 In what ways might the 'Agnes and Charlie' story support and challenge evolution?
15 Why might some argue that evolution is a theory and others that it is a fact?
16 What would count as evidence supporting and/or rejecting evolution?
17 Why might Darwin have been troubled by his theory of evolution?
18 Describe how geological evidence led Darwin to question creation by God.
19 What conclusions did Darwin draw from the fossil record?

20 How did Darwin's voyage on HMS *Beagle* add to his thinking about evolution?
21 In what ways is pigeon breeding linked to Darwin's emerging theory of evolution?
22 What are the likely mechanisms of evolution?
23 How is DNA linked to evolution?
24 What possible questions remain about evolution?
25 Explain one way in which someone might respond to evolution.

Analyse and Evaluate

1 Compare different scientific responses to Big Bang theory.
2 In what ways might Big Bang theory challenge religious views about the origins of the universe?
3 'Science argues that Big Bang theory is the best explanation we currently have for the origins of the universe but a best explanation is not enough.' Discuss.
4 'The only reasonable explanation for the origins of the universe is Big Bang theory.' Discuss this claim.
5 Analyse the view that 'the scientific evidence available today can only point to the Big Bang as the explanation of the origins of the universe'.
6 'The evidence supporting Darwin's theory of evolution is overwhelming and compelling.' Discuss this claim.
7 Analyse the view that Darwin's own reaction to evolutionary theory is not relevant to the truth or otherwise of the theory.
8 'Evolution provides the best fit for the available evidence. That is enough.' Discuss.
9 'Evolution explains how life on Earth began and developed, but it does not explain why.' Discuss.

Big Bang explains the how and whit, the when, the whaur, oh aye

But disna dae much o' a job in sayin' much aboot why

Aye, time began and matter tae, aw in a great Big Stooshie

But no a word aboot a'body that might huv given it a push – eh?

Cos aw that maths and aw that physics fair does ma heid in guid

I hivna a clue whit it aw means and wouldna care if I did

I dinna ken much aboot the Big Man either, for mibbee it wis his role

Tae make a universe that big and make mankind wi' a soul

Ye see, I get the scientific stuff, and think they're aw dead smart

But makin' a human isny a science, it's much merr like an art

And as fur comin' straight fae chimps you're surely huvin a laugh

Why no just make us as we are withoot the messy faff

Yon Darwin wis a bright wan tae, an' likely a decent chap

But his theory's tough and hard tae get and makes me want tae nap

But then, I'm no the brightest, no the sharpest knife on the block

So it's no ma place tae take a swipe, tae giggle or tae mock

They've worked dead hard these scientists, tae come up wi' that stuff

So mibbee I'll just play along and tell them 'fair enough'

Ye ken yer stuff, ye ken yer facts, yer aw that flippin' bright

So I'll just take it as ye say and smile and say 'yer right' (in a way)

For I'm bamboozled by yer words, yer sums, yer graphs and tables

So I'll just stick wi whit I think – even though they might be fables

For it's my faith that tells me whit's the right response tae take

An' if I'm wrang then fair enough, it willna make me ache

Nae need for fancy logic, claims or reason

I'll make ma ain decisions thanks, it's no exactly treason

Compatibility

The issues surrounding the origins of the universe and of life can be approached from a religious perspective or from a non-religious perspective. Within each perspective there can be agreement, disagreement and, perhaps eventually, some kind of compatibility – although compatibility isn't always possible, especially around topics which can generate very strong views, such as this. In addition, of course, religious and non-religious perspectives can also agree, disagree and reach some kind of compatibility – though you'll have to decide for yourself if you think it is easier for religious and non-religious people to reach a position of compatibility or for different kinds of religious people to reach one. You have to be aware that it's not as simple as science on one side and religion on the other, but the question we have to answer is whether it is possible or not to accept both scientific and religious explanations for the origins of the universe and life.

We also need to ask if all religious explanations for the origins of the universe and life are compatible with each other. There are two things to consider here. First, within a religion there may be disagreements about origins and therefore different views which may not always be compatible. Second, there may be different views about origins across different religions which may not always be compatible.

Compatibility within a religion

Even within one religion, there can be major disagreements about the origins of the universe and life. Some religious people within one religion may take a very literal approach to interpreting creation stories – believing them to be literally true as recorded in their scriptures. Others within the same religion might take a very liberal approach to the same scriptures, seeing them not as literal truth but as metaphors and symbols. So, within Christianity, for example, some will believe that there was literally one Adam and Eve, the first humans tempted by a serpent, while others might believe that these first 'two' were simply representations of the first humans (of which there were many). Some Christians will argue that humans were created exactly as they appear now, while others will allow for the possibility that the human species has developed according to the broad principles of evolution.

Compatibility across religions

This is going to produce very different levels of agreement, disagreement and, possibly, compatibility. For example, there is considerable agreement about the details of the creation story across Judaism, Christianity and Islam, while between these three religions and Hinduism there are considerable disagreements. The nature of each religion will be very closely linked to how far one religion can agree with another. For example, Judaism, Islam and Christianity are monotheistic religions – believing in the existence of one God, and a God who is the creator. Buddhism, on the other hand, is a religion which does not have a central divine figure and so there is no possibility of any divine creator. Therefore between monotheistic and non-monotheistic religions there is likely to be significant disagreement about the origins of the universe and of life, and very little chance of reaching any kind of compatibility.

Talk Point

Is disagreement healthy or harmful within a religion?

4 CAN RELIGIOUS AND SCIENTIFIC VIEWS ON ORIGINS BE COMPATIBLE?

43

Are all non-religious explanations for the origins of the universe and life compatible with each other?

Similarly, non-religious people, groups and philosophies might disagree about the origins of life and the universe. One key difference here is that the agreement or disagreement is likely to be based on different understandings of evidence. Non-religious perspectives tend to stress the importance of making decisions based on reason and evidence – and reaching logical conclusions based on this. However, interpreting evidence is a very human activity, and while the evidence around evolution and Big Bang theory is what it is, interpreting it can result in very different conclusions being reached. For non-religious people, such disagreement is a strength which is, in fact, the basis for their approach to life – you gather the evidence, find what is the best fit for a theory and that becomes what you accept – until new evidence comes along (or new ways of looking at old evidence) and you adjust your thinking accordingly.

It is also important to remember that with non-religious perspectives there is often no central teaching/line/viewpoint to which all who share the perspective are expected to subscribe. For example, it is perhaps more appropriate to say there are views about the origins of the universe to which a Humanist may or may not subscribe, than to say there is a Humanist view about it.

Compatibility between religious and non-religious perspectives

Compatibility between religious and non-religious perspectives isn't necessarily as simple as 'either/or'. Of course, some religious perspectives will have completely opposite views about the origins of life and the universe compared to non-religious perspectives. However, it's perhaps better to think of this as a continuum with varying degrees of agreement and disagreement along the way – points of compatibility if you like. For example, a religious person might accept the details of evolution and the evidence pointing to it, but still argue that the cause of this was God. However, for some there are going to be non-negotiable beliefs which will lead to incompatibility between perspectives. For example, a religious person may believe that when all is said and done, the universe and life were created by God – no matter what technique or method he used – while for a non-religious person this would be an unacceptable position since God is not a verifiable or falsifiable concept.

Talk Point

How far do you think compatibility is possible between religious and non-religious perspectives on the origins of life and the universe?

Does it matter how the universe began?

Most people probably don't choose to discuss the origins of the universe while tucking in to their tea. However, for many people it is an important question to consider because of the potential implications of one explanation as opposed to another.

▶ For religious people, how the universe began is an important piece of evidence for their belief in God. Their scriptures tell them how the universe began and science seems to say something different, so it is important for religious people to try to reconcile this as best they can.

▶ For religious people, life, the universe and everything in it has meaning and purpose because, in their view, they were created by God. If the universe is a simple consequence of the laws of physics, this could bring into question the purpose of life. Of course, non-religious people find meaning in life without a God. If there was no need for a God to bring the universe into existence then perhaps other evidence for God's existence might be wrong, too, and this would have serious implications for religious belief.

- For non-religious people, understanding the origin of the universe is part of our human drive to explain things and, like every other viewpoint and belief, it should be based on evidence. For some non-religious people, accepting things by faith is a dangerous approach to life because, they argue, it makes humans content to live without seeking answers.
- Some non-religious people feel that religion does a lot of harm, and anything which can discredit it (such as demonstrating that the universe needed no creator) is not a bad thing. On the other hand, religious people tend to believe that religion is a force for good and so believing that God brought about the universe is a good thing.

Non-religious responses to Big Bang theory

There are three possible responses to Big Bang theory as an explanation for the origin of the universe. One is that it is wrong, one is that it is right, and the third is that it is some complex mixture of the two. Which position you take will determine the extent to which you might agree or disagree with other non-religious people or, indeed, religious people, and therefore the extent to which compatibility of beliefs/viewpoints is possible.

Big Bang theory is wrong

Some may well reject Big Bang theory because they think the evidence does not point to the universe beginning with a Big Bang. They may take the view that there is conflicting evidence which seems more probable. However, it's likely that such people are few and far between, since evidence which goes against Big Bang theory is hard to find. However, those who reject Big Bang theory may do so not because they dispute the evidence, but because they dispute the *interpretation* of the evidence. They might argue that while the evidence is what it is, the conclusions which have been drawn from it are not accurate. Some may go further, arguing that science is not as neutral, objective and value-free as it appears to be. They might say that scientists bring pre-existing views about things to the evidence they analyse, and that this means they analyse the evidence in one way rather than another – leading to one conclusion rather than another. They're probably not suggesting that scientists do this intentionally, but that it is an unavoidable consequence of being a human being.

Others might argue that there are issues about the empirical verifiability/falsifiability of Big Bang theory which make it suspect. The available evidence may well point to the universe beginning as Big Bang theory states, but in reality there is no way to demonstrate beyond doubt that it happened this way. All our projections about the first few moments of the universe are exactly that – projections based on assumptions. No one was there to witness it and no one can go back to do so. Therefore what we have is evidence that it is most likely to have happened as described, but philosophically that is not the same thing as being able to say that it *did* happen as described.

Some may reject Big Bang theory because the evidence, in their view, is inconclusive. Some of the anomalies with the evidence we have (for example, the uneven distribution of matter throughout the universe) mean that it is not enough to accept Big Bang theory until these anomalies are explained – the stakes are too high. If you are going to attempt to explain the origin of the universe, perhaps all your evidence should be complete and watertight. Of course, a response might be that, in science, evidence is often incomplete but we build the best explanatory model we can based on the evidence we have – until better evidence (or better ways of explaining the evidence) arrives.

As mentioned earlier, some people may reject Big Bang theory on the basis that it makes no logical sense to say that at some point in time there was no such thing as time, and somewhere where there was nothing. These seem logically contradictory and, although physicists can make these theoretical claims, logically speaking they are so hard to grasp that perhaps they call into question Big Bang theory. Along with this, some might reject Big Bang theory because, although it might explain the 'how' of the beginning of the universe, it leaves other questions unanswered. They might argue, for example, that the change in state from no universe to a universe is not explained – what caused the Big Bang remains unclear – and this sticking point may raise doubts about the overall theory. Some, of course, respond that the question 'What caused the Big Bang?' is an invalid question entirely. The debate goes on.

4 CAN RELIGIOUS AND SCIENTIFIC VIEWS ON ORIGINS BE COMPATIBLE?

45

Big Bang theory is right

There's not much to say about this. This takes the view that the evidence for the Big Bang is accurate and compelling and does point to it as the explanation for the beginning of the universe. It might well be a 'best fit' for the evidence argument – but that is enough. Yes, there may be some logical difficulties about no time before time and so on, but if the science points to that, then perhaps we just have to adapt philosophically to such concepts, even though they are not nice and neat. This approach may also take into account possible alternative theories, from science or religion, and dismiss them for various reasons. For example, philosophically speaking, accepting the existence of an uncreated creator is no more reasonable than accepting the existence of an uncreated universe. Proposing a God as an explanation for the origin of the universe just creates a new problem – the requirement for an explanation for the origin of God. Since non-religious perspectives tend to value evidence and reason as opposed to belief alone, conclusions will be reached about Big Bang theory based on interpretation of the available evidence.

Compatibility across non-religious perspectives

It is likely that non-religious people will be able to reach a position of some degree of compatibility, since for them weighing up the evidence is how you arrive at beliefs. This doesn't mean that interpretations of the evidence within non-religious perspectives won't lead to heated debate, just that the importance given to such debate within non-religious perspectives is likely to be different from its place in religious perspectives. Non-religious perspectives will take the view that the constant search for evidence and the constant reinterpretation of evidence is a good thing and is what leads to progress. Believing something to be right or wrong just because you do is not really meant to have a place in such thinking. (Of course, that's not to say it doesn't happen.) Therefore, non-religious people are likely to be able to agree to a certain degree of compatibility in the conclusion they draw about the origin of the universe.

Talk Point

Do you think it is easier to find some degree of compatibility within non-religious perspectives than within religious ones?

Religious responses to Big Bang theory

Big Bang theory is wrong

Rejecting Big Bang theory on the basis of belief may well draw upon some of the ideas held by those who reject it based on evidence. They, too, might reject the evidence or the manner in which it is interpreted, the gaps in the evidence or the logical implausibility of many aspects of the theory. However, it is likely that they will reject the theory because of their belief in a completely different explanation for the origin of the universe – creation by God. There will be different levels of literal understanding of this. Some will argue that God created the universe as the first chapter of Genesis describes it: in six days, in a particular order and so on. So their response to Big Bang theory is simple: it cannot be true because it contradicts the biblical version of events – and as the Bible is the inspired word of God, then the Bible must be true and Big Bang theory wrong. This response is likely to come from those who take the biblical creation story as literally true.

Some might add that the creation of the universe by God adds something very important which Big Bang theory does not include: purpose. In their view, the idea that the universe began for no reason other than the blind laws of physics is not satisfactory. They would argue that the universe must have a reason and a purpose – which they would claim is more likely if it was created purposely by God. (There are different views about what this purpose might be.) Those who reject this claim could well argue that the desire of religious people for a universe with purpose does not mean that it has any such thing – nor needs to. In fact, any purpose in the existence of the universe does not make sense – and the evidence presented by Big Bang theory might be taken to contradict it. For example, stars die and new ones are born all the time in the universe – what was their purpose? Creatures are eaten by other creatures – was the purpose of the creature which was eaten simply to be eaten by something else? Besides, arguing that the universe must have purpose, and that the Big Bang does not explain what this purpose might be, does not therefore mean that everything about Big Bang theory is wrong. Those who argue that God created the universe, rather than the universe 'created itself', need to explain the origin of God. To argue that God needs no origin while the universe does, is contradictory, but this approach by religious people is based on faith – their belief in the truth of a religious explanation for the origin of the universe. Remember that this 'faith' might also take into account evidence in support of religious belief too.

Big Bang theory is right

Yes, there are religious people who accept Big Bang theory completely as an explanation for the origin of the universe. Their argument is simple: science deals with what can be measured, observed and explained using evidence. Religion deals with the unmeasurable, what is unable to be observed, and has no automatic requirement for evidence. This means that some religious people can effectively keep their religious beliefs in one compartment of their mind, so to speak, and scientific explanations in another. This means that they can accept Big Bang theory while simultaneously accepting their religious beliefs about the origin of the universe. In short, you can accept all the scientific explanations for the Big Bang and still think it was God who made it happen.

Compatibility

Across religions, 'compatibility' might simply mean each religion accepts its own teaching and rejects that of another. This might not seem like compatibility but you could regard it as being true to your own faith while not necessarily criticising someone else's – and as long as you can live together harmoniously in disagreement, what's the problem? Of course, some religious perspectives might feel compatibility is impossible either across or within religions, since there is a 'true' and a 'false' answer to how the universe began and you have to choose one side or the other. Some religious people accept the possibility that there are different ways of understanding scriptures, even within a religious tradition (or that scriptures can speak of one thing in one religion which might be applicable in another, though expressed differently). Alternatively, within and between religions, and between religious and non-religious perspectives, you could simply hold that both Big Bang theory and religious explanations are *simultaneously* true.

Compatibility between religious and scientific perspectives

Let's look more closely at how religious people can accept both Big Bang theory and religious explanations for the origin of the universe.

- **Big Bang theory and religious beliefs occupy different 'domains'.** Science approaches things in one way and religion in another. As long as both keep to their own approaches and methods, there need not be any conflict. This may depend on how literally you take religious accounts of the origins of the universe. Some non-religious people might reject this approach because they argue that you cannot put things in a box in this way. In fact, they might go further and say that 'sitting on the fence' in this way is dangerous – because it allows anyone to disregard hard evidence which does not match their religious explanations.
- **Big Bang theory explains the mechanism of God's creation.** Perhaps Big Bang theory is the way in which God created the universe – perhaps, in fact, science is giving us incredible insight into the creative activity of God in the beginning. There is nothing in the Bible which goes into any detail about the actual methods used by God in the beginning – so there's nothing to stop a religious person believing that the Big Bang was the way 'God did it'. This, of course, is another response based on faith and belief. There's no real meeting ground between religious and non-religious views on this because it is a matter of faith and faith alone. Non-religious people might argue that

4 CAN RELIGIOUS AND SCIENTIFIC VIEWS ON ORIGINS BE COMPATIBLE?

47

science has provided many scientific explanations for things which used to have religious explanations – so why not Big Bang for the origin of the universe without the need for a God?

▸ **Evidence of Big Bang theory is inconclusive.** Some religious people might argue that the evidence for Big Bang theory has gaps and that this calls into question the overall theory, or allows you to 'slot in' a creator God. Of course, non-religious people would respond that such gaps are normal in science – and also what would religious people do if all the gaps were filled with scientific answers? Besides, even if Big Bang theory was demonstrated to be 100 per cent wrong tomorrow, it does not automatically follow that the alternative explanation for the origin of the universe must be creation by God.

▸ **Big Bang theory explains the 'how, what, when and where' of the origins of the universe but not the 'why'.** For many religious people, the apparent meaninglessness of the Big Bang explanation is a problem. If everything is just the result of the laws of physics, then what does this say about any purpose of life? Some religious people therefore take the view that science explains the facts, but religion gives them their meaning. Non-religious people might respond by questioning the need for any 'meaning' for the universe – perhaps it just *is*. And, they might argue, even if the universe did have some kind of meaning, why would any such meaning only be able to be explained in a religious way? Perhaps life in the universe has meaning regardless of whether there was a creator God or not. And perhaps the question about meaning is itself meaningless in relation to the truth or otherwise of Big Bang theory.

Of course, non-religious people are unlikely to accept most of this 'compatibility', since their belief is based on the view that there is no God and therefore no creator. However, some might argue that since the existence of God is neither verifiable nor falsifiable, then it is not a fit topic for non-religious people to comment upon. Therefore 'compatibility' could be possible if it means simply agreeing to disagree.

Does it matter how life on Earth began?

For some religious and non-religious people there is little point in thinking about how life on Earth began, but for some it is a very important question because of the possible implications that it raises for belief.

▸ For many religious people, humans are a special part of creation – God's greatest achievement. If the beginning of life on Earth was down to 'just' the blind laws of chance, it would mean humans are perhaps not that special after all. However, many people, religious and non-religious, might argue that humans are something special – no matter how they originated.

▸ Whether life on Earth was created by God or by the chance laws of evolution is important to many people because if evolution is true then it could call into question aspects of the biblical creation story, and therefore of creation by God. In fact, it might well call into question God's existence entirely – and this is clearly an issue for religious people.

▸ Religious people argue that life has meaning and purpose and that God has his reasons for things. Evolutionary processes simply respond to environmental ones and for religious people that shows a lack of purpose, and goes against their view that God has a plan for everyone and everything.

▸ For non-religious people there is an issue about accepting the creation of life on Earth as a matter of faith, not evidence. In their view, such an approach holds back human development and leaves us open to all the dangers of superstition based on lack of evidence.

Non-religious responses to evolution

Evolution may not be the full story...

As for responses to the Big Bang, the challenge here is not about the scientific evidence, but more about the interpretation of the evidence, and the approach involved in scientific method. Interpreting evidence is not done in a cultural, moral and social bubble and perhaps people might bring with them their own personal baggage when approaching the evidence for evolution. It certainly seems to be the case that the more accepted a theory becomes, the less easy it is to challenge it.

To claim that the evidence shows that evolution must be the mechanism for the origin/development of life on Earth is not the same as saying it *was*. The evidence may point to evolution being true but that's not, philosophically speaking, the same thing as saying that it is true.

Some may argue that the gaps in the evidence for evolution suggest the possibility that it might not be completely accurate. However, although there are gaps in the evidence, this does not mean that any other competing explanation for the origin and development of life on Earth must therefore be right. Any competing claim would need to provide its own evidence and that would have to be better than the evidence for evolution. Some might reject evolution based on reason because they might argue that it explains the biology of the development of life on Earth but not the purpose. The argument might be that while science can explain the physical development of life on Earth, this says nothing about its purpose or meaning. Some may go further and argue that – in relation to human beings, at any rate – there is something 'more to us' than biology. Evolution may explain our physical development, but science can say nothing about the existence of our consciousness, self-awareness, or the possible existence of a spiritual dimension to our lives. Scientists could, of course, respond that science is now able to comment about consciousness and complex neurological processes which may account for those things which have been considered non-physical for a long time. They may also argue that life on Earth needs no ultimate 'meaning', or that we each make our own 'meaning of life' – so this is hardly any reason to reject evolution.

Evolution is right

As for Big Bang theory, there is little to say here. This takes the view that evolution is both reasonable and based on reliable and valid evidence which is both verifiable and falsifiable in principle (as well as in practice, in some instances). Also, any religious alternatives to evolution would still have to provide evidence or arguments to support their view that life on Earth was created but that a divine creator does not need to be created. This is logically contradictory. In general, it is safe to argue that non-religious perspectives accept evolution as the correct account of the origin and development of life on Earth. This is because non-religious perspectives base their views on evidence and the view is that the evidence is overwhelmingly in support of evolution.

Compatibility

As for Big Bang theory, it is likely that the issues with 'compatibility' in this situation mean the way in which you interpret the evidence. There may remain minor details of disagreement across non-religious perspectives about evolution but these will be very minor: the vast majority of non-religious perspectives will have no disagreement about the general principle of evolution.

Religious responses to evolution

Evolution is wrong

Many of the same arguments which apply to rejection of Big Bang theory based on religious belief also apply to evolution. In order to simplify the arguments we will consider views within Christianity. First of all, there are some major arguments:

- Evolution seems to contradict what is revealed in scripture
- So evolution seems to do away with the need for God
- Evolution is not driven by any being but is simply driven by a series of random changes. This goes against belief in a divine creator with a purpose
- Since evolution is a series of random, chance events, this calls into question beliefs that life has a meaning and a purpose

4 CAN RELIGIOUS AND SCIENTIFIC VIEWS ON ORIGINS BE COMPATIBLE?

49

Biblical creationism

Firstly, some reject evolution simply because it conflicts with the biblical account of the creation of life. The Bible describes how life on Earth began and, for biblical creationists, the Bible is the literal word of God, therefore all the apparent evidence for evolution must be wrong. This is straightforward biblical creationism and it tends not to go into any scientific arguments about the evidence for and against evolution – it simply accepts that the biblical story is enough evidence against the truth of evolution. This belief can apply no matter how literally the religious person regards the creation story. Non-religious people tend to reject this approach by arguing that the evidence for evolution cannot be ignored and certainly not in favour of an ancient myth. They argue that something is not true just because you believe it to be true.

Talk Point

Do you think there are any strong arguments for rejecting evolution?

Intelligent design and creation science

Some creationists go further and use arguments based on intelligent design and creation science. These take a two-pronged approach to attacking evolution, based on the overarching belief that the origin of the universe and life on Earth must be the result of creation by an intelligent designer and that there is evidence to support this. Intelligent design and creation science first challenges the accuracy and completeness of the evidence for evolution and, second, offers its own conflicting evidence.

The challenges to the evidence for evolution are based on the view that the evidence is incomplete and incorrectly interpreted. Intelligent design and creation science takes the view that:

▸ **The idea that life originated and developed by chance is unacceptable.** There must be greater purpose to life than the blind and random forces of evolution, and religious explanations provide accounts of that purpose. Non-religious people may respond that there is no need for 'purpose' in life, and/ or that evolution provides its own purpose, and/or that even if life does need purpose, this does not support any need for a divine creator.

▸ **Inorganic matter cannot become organic matter.** Any 'evidence' which supports this idea is flawed. Responses to this might be that laboratory experiments to recreate conditions on early Earth are perfectly reasonable and their findings accurate. Again, even if inorganic matter could not become organic matter, that does not mean that the origin of organic life on Earth must be explained by the existence of a God.

▸ **Common descent of life on Earth because of similarities could just as easily be explained by common design.** Of course, this cuts both ways, and concluding that evolution is wrong is just a point of view and nothing more.

▸ **The fossil record is incomplete.** One major criticism of evolution from proponents of intelligent design and creation science is that the fossil record does not show all the stages of the development of life on Earth. A response to this would be that such evidence may yet be discovered, or may not, but a theory cannot be rejected because of the absence of every piece of evidence.

▸ **Irreducible complexity is an argument against evolution.** Advocates of intelligent design and creation science argue that organisms are systems which require all of their parts to be there to contribute to their basic functions; if you take away something from this (therefore reducing its complexity) then you no longer have the organism. Evolution's idea that living things gradually develop into more complex ones is therefore flawed. Proponents of intelligent design and creation science say that this further supports intelligent design by a divine creator. Responses to this argue that each successive addition to an organism confers some advantage on it (for example, the light-sensitive cells mentioned in Chapter 3) and that irreducible complexity is another example of circular logic – starting with a belief in a creator God, disputing evidence for evolution and then suggesting this must point to a creator God. (And, of course, even if it did, it might be any kind of creator, not necessarily the same one that those who believe in intelligent design and creation science generally believe in.)

Talk Point

Should religious people use science to support their beliefs?

Evolution is right

For many religious people, evolution and belief in a creator God are not contradictory. They might take the view that evolution explains the scientific mechanism of the development of life on Earth, while religion offers them something about the meaning and purpose of life on Earth. Evolution is a valid argument for the development of life on Earth, and it does not offer any evidence directly *against* belief in God.

Compatibility

For many religious people, it is perfectly possible to accept that evolution is true and that creation by God is true as well.

▸ As for the Big Bang, evolution and religious belief occupy different domains. The view is taken that evolution explains the biological mechanism for the origin and development of life on Earth, while religion offers explanation about its meaning, direction and purpose. Religion should not try to disprove the claims of science because it is not equipped to do so. In the same way, science should not try to disprove the claims of religion since it does not have the techniques to do so. Again, non-religious people might argue that treating religion and science as two equally valid ways to explain things is not a useful or defendable position to take.

▸ Perhaps evolution is simply God's way of creating and developing life on Earth. The Bible doesn't claim to be a science book and so perhaps the creation story might be true in one way, while evolution is true in another. In fact, many religious people would actually welcome the claims of evolution, because they would feel that this helps us to better understand the way in which God began and developed life on Earth. Non-religious people might argue that evolution provides evidence that a creator God is unnecessary, and so this idea of holding on to both explanations doesn't make sense. Besides, evolution points to a 'blind' process where chance mutations do or do not thrive in chance changes to environments. How, they might argue, does this fit with the idea of an all-powerful, all-good God who has 'a plan'?

▸ Some religious people might argue that the gaps in evidence for evolution allow them to 'find space' for God, though few would be likely to take this unpredictable 'God of the gaps' approach. This is because their view would need to be amended every time a gap was filled – and what kind of faith does that represent?

4 CAN RELIGIOUS AND SCIENTIFIC VIEWS ON ORIGINS BE COMPATIBLE?

51

▶ Many religious people reject intelligent design and creation science for the same reason. First, they might take the view that faith does not need the evidence or argument that intelligent design and creation science so carefully and exhaustively seeks. Second, they might argue that intelligent design and creation science sets itself up to be disproved by the very techniques it supports.

▶ Finally, some religious people argue that while evolution explains the origin and development of life on Earth, their religious faith gives them meaning and purpose in life. Of course, non-religious people will claim that life can have purpose and meaning even if evolution is true and that any meaning in life does not need any divine origin of life.

Compatibility between religious and non-religious perspectives

There are deeply held views on both sides of the argument and some people are likely to argue that compatibility between religious and non-religious perspectives is never possible, since for one explanation to be true, the other must be false – they can't both contain truth. Alternatively, some people argue that compatibility is possible, if you take a different approach to what 'true' might mean. This goes back to literal and metaphorical interpretations of evidence and stories which could lead some to think that evolution and creation are simultaneously true – albeit in different ways.

Personal Reflection

* *Have any of your views about the Big Bang and/or evolution changed while considering this topic?*
* *Do you think life has meaning? If so, what is this meaning?*
* *What might be the benefits and drawbacks of religious and non-religious perspectives on the Big Bang/evolution 'minding their own business'?*

Apply your learning

Active Learning

1 Prepare a list of questions you would ask the following people: someone who supports Big Bang theory based on non-religious grounds, someone who supports Big Bang theory based on religious grounds and someone who rejects Big Bang theory. Pass these questions to another group who have the task of responding to them.

2 One minute speed-dating: choose one of the positions/viewpoints about the Big Bang or evolution you have considered in this chapter. Now, in a speed-dating format, you must speak to someone else in your class about this position/viewpoint for one minute without stopping.

3 In the form of a rhyming poem, script a conversation between two religious people, one of whom believes in evolution and one who does not.

4 Create a series of questions for a quiz-show format of your choice based on the arguments in this chapter. You could then run the quiz show in your class.

Investigate

Find out more about:

➤ religious and non-religious views about 'life's meaning'
➤ claims and counter-claims about intelligent design and creation science
➤ responses from religious people about intelligent design and creation science
➤ well-known scientists who combine science with their religious belief
➤ scientists who argue that religious belief holds back human development.

For each of these, report your findings in a manner of your choice. This could be a written report or presentation – in the form of tables, graphs and charts – or as the source of material for a class debate or discussion. You should select a method for your report which is most appropriate for the aspect you are investigating.

Check Your Understanding

1 Describe how someone might reject Big Bang theory based on religious belief.
2 Describe how someone might reject Big Bang theory based on non-religious belief.
3 How might a religious person accept Big Bang theory as true by arguing that religious and non-religious perspectives occupy different 'domains'?
4 Explain two ways in which a religious person might be able to accept the Big Bang as true.
5 Why might a non-religious person reject evolution?
6 Explain two of the main claims of intelligent design and creation science.
7 Why might a religious person reject the claims of intelligent design and creation science?
8 What is meant by 'God of the gaps' and how might a religious person respond to this?
9 Explain how a religious person might accept evolution and creation by God simultaneously.
10 Describe one possible criticism of someone who accepts evolution and creation as both being true.
11 Why might a religious person argue that the 'meaning' of life is important in this debate, and how might a non-religious person respond?
12 Is compatibility between religious and non-religious perspectives ever possible?

Analyse and Evaluate

1 'Religious and non-religious people will never agree on the origin of human life.' Discuss.
2 Analyse the view that intelligent design and creation science is a valid way to respond to the claims of science about there being no need for a creator.
3 'While religion claims to provide meaning for life on Earth, it can do so no more than non-religious perspectives.' Discuss.
4 To what extent are religious and non-religious beliefs about the origin and development of the universe/life on Earth compatible?

EXISTENCE
OF GOD: DOES
GOD EXIST?

Religious arguments, theories and evidence

5

DISHTOWELS ➡ ①

Unless you are lucky enough to have a dishwasher, you may occasionally be called upon to dry the dishes. Of course, even if you have a dishwasher, some parents might argue that some dishes take up too much space in the dishwasher, or that the 'nice glasses' have to be washed and dried by hand so they don't get all cloudy. (They'll probably say such things soon after telling you that you spend far too much time on your phone and enquiring if you are really going out dressed like that …) So, inevitably, and perhaps with a heavy heart, you pick up the dish towel to dry up every now and again (perhaps under parental instruction on pain of not getting any pocket money). Now at this point, as a good RMPS student, you should be asking some questions about this dish towel: how many dish towels have there been throughout Earth's history and, most importantly, what did the first dish towel look like? In fact, you might reach the conclusion that there had to be a first ever dish towel – perhaps one that was invented by a very clever dish-towel maker, and that all the dish towels after this one were modified versions of this first dish towel. On the other hand, perhaps there never was a 'first dish towel'. Perhaps something has always been used to dry the dishes – for as long as there have been dishes to dry. Perhaps there was no notion of a dish towel way back in time, but instead simply a cloth which dried dishes (although it's hard to see how that would differ from a dish towel). So, was there a point when the first dish towel came into being? Did someone invent it? Or was there never a point at which the first dish towel appeared on the scene, just a series of things which dried dishes stretching back to infinity?

Talk Point

Do you think that there needs to have been a first version of everything which exists?

Why does the cause of the universe matter to many people?

We will look at four of the many different versions of the cosmological argument but first it is important to understand why having an understanding of the beginning of the universe matters to people. For many religious and non-religious people alike, it matters because people like to understand things – it is part of human nature. For religious people, believing that the universe had a cause in the form of God helps them with their view that life has meaning and purpose. If the universe has always existed or come into being spontaneously without any need for a divine creator, then perhaps there's no real purpose to it all. Non-religious people find their meaning and purpose without the need for a God and for them an eternal universe or one which came into being without any creator is still the same universe – and the meaning and purpose of their life is still the same.

You should be aware, too, that for some religious people, arguments about the cause of the universe are not especially important – this is because their belief is based on faith, not reason, and so their view that God was the first cause is a matter of faith, unaffected by evidence and/or argument. Some, in fact, don't spend any time thinking about issues like this – preferring to live their lives according to their beliefs, perhaps leaving such questions to people studying RMPS.

Some non-religious people get irritated by the argument that things should just be accepted on faith. This is because they feel that this holds back humanity from seeking answers and assessing the evidence, and so has negative consequences for our species. Many religious people respond that in cases like the origin of the universe, the evidence is always going to be open for debate – whether that is scientific evidence or philosophical arguments about the origins of the universe.

These ideas can all be reduced to something quite simple. If the cosmological argument is correct then it offers strong logical support for belief in God. If, however, it is a flawed argument then it does not support belief in God and, in fact, might count against belief in God.

Talk Point

How much does the origin of the universe matter to you?

Religious arguments, theories and evidence: the cosmological argument

There are many versions of this argument. It is an argument that has been used throughout the ages to attempt to prove the necessity of a first cause for the existence of everything that we see around us. Sometimes it has been used to support belief in the existence of a divine creator not linked to any specific faith or religious group, while at other times it has been used to support belief in the existence of a particular creator from a particular religion.

The argument rests on logic and is based upon the observable reality of everything there is. A series of premises build into a complete argument in support of the existence of a divine creator/creators/God/gods. The argument is based on what philosophers call *a posteriori* ('what comes after') knowledge – where the process of reasoning is applied to what has been observed or experienced in order to explain why it happened. More specifically, this is *inductive reasoning*, where the existence of a divine creator is inferred from what has been observed/experienced. The argument is sometimes referred to as the First Cause argument or the 'argument from causation'.

1 The cosmological argument from Plato

Plato (around 427–347 BCE) was a Greek philosopher (one of the first recorded philosophers). (He is included here in the religious arguments section because his was probably one of the first cosmological arguments and it was built upon and adapted by religious individuals and groups.) He argued in *Laws* (Sections 893–896) as follows:

▶ The universe and everything in it is in a constant state of change.
▶ Each change is caused by a previous change.
▶ Working backwards, the chain of causes of change would have to go back infinitely.
▶ Such a situation is not logically possible – change cannot go back infinitely, with change causing change, without any initial cause for change.
▶ Therefore there must have been a cause for the first change.
▶ That cause must itself not have been caused by anything else.

Plato did not argue that this first cause was any specific God, or even (any specific) one of the gods, instead referring to this first mover as 'soul' or 'life'.

Strengths of Plato's argument

Perhaps the main strength of Plato's argument is that it is not based on a statement of faith (such as 'I believe it so it must be true'). Plato tried to use logic and reasoning to provide evidence for the existence of a divine creator, since more concrete evidence about a divine creator is less apparent than it could be. One way to look at his argument is as a form of intellectual circumstantial evidence. Of course, it could be argued that if there was a divine creator, he/she/it could easily make their existence known and then there would be no need for argument, though this would, perhaps, raise some issues in relation to free will, which we will explore elsewhere.

Weaknesses of Plato's argument

Like all the cosmological arguments, Plato's argument suffers from what philosophers refer to as a fallacy – or error – in its reasoning. In his argument, Plato takes the view that an infinite series of regressions of change causing change is not logically possible. There are three obvious problems with this.

1   This is an assumption made by Plato in the absence of evidence. Why should it be impossible for there to be an infinite series of regressions without any first cause? Perhaps it is perfectly reasonable (and true) that the causes go back infinitely.
2   Even if it were logically impossible, that is not the same as it being impossible in reality.
3   Plato argues that everything needs a cause. Why does this have to be so? Plato observed that things in nature need a cause and this led him to the conclusion that everything must have a cause. However, this does not need to be the case. Just because the things Plato knew about needed causes does not mean the things he did not know about also needed causes. On what basis did he assume that they too must have causes?

Another weakness of Plato's argument could be linked to his conclusion that any first cause had to have particular characteristics. Plato defined this first cause in ways which are understandable for his listeners, using words like *soul*, *life* and *demiurge*. (Demiurge is a word which means 'creator'.) However, even if there had to be some first cause, Plato's argument does nothing to tell us anything meaningful about the nature of this first cause. Like all cosmological arguments, Plato has assumed that an actual conclusion in reality can be inferred from a series of arguments which only exist in the mind – and many reject this form of reasoning.

Talk Point

What do you think of Plato's argument and the responses to it?

2 The cosmological argument from Thomas Aquinas

Thomas Aquinas (1225–1274) was a member of the Dominican religious order, and made a saint in the fourteenth century. Aquinas' argument is very similar to Plato's. However, Aquinas takes it one step further to support his belief in a specific God – the God of Christianity in whom he believed. Aquinas' cosmological argument is as follows:

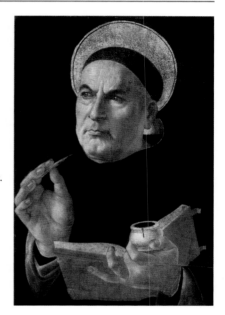

▶ We can observe that the universe and everything in it exists.
▶ Everything which exists must have a cause for its existence (something which came before it and which caused it – and this makes everything *contingent* upon other things).
▶ There must have been, at some point in time, a first cause for every other cause.
▶ This first cause must, by definition, be an uncaused being (since an infinite series of causes makes no sense) – and this would make such a being a *necessary* being).
▶ The only possible thing which could be uncaused would be God.
▶ Therefore, the first uncaused cause must be God.
▶ So God must exist.

Strengths of Aquinas' argument

Like Plato, Aquinas used logical reasoning to support something which was otherwise a statement of faith. However, while Plato's argument pointed to a generic divine being, Aquinas used his argument to support the existence of a divine being who could only be the God that he and other Christians believed in. This was perhaps an attempt to direct the argument away from the conclusion that any divine creature was responsible for creation, and instead towards supporting the whole package of the Judaeo-Christian God.

Weaknesses of Aquinas' argument

Aquinas combined his faith with reason to produce what he felt was a reasonable, logical explanation for something he believed anyway. However, there are some potential problems with his argument.

1 Starting with a pre-existing belief (God created the universe) perhaps introduces an element of 'confirmation bias' into Aquinas' argument. In other words, perhaps he was more inclined to accept arguments which supported his belief in God rather than anything which might question it.
2 Some have argued, against Aquinas (and against all versions of the cosmological argument), that observing that things exist is just a way of interpreting our senses. Perhaps things do not, in fact, have real existence 'out there' but instead everything which appears to exist does so only in our mind. If this is so, then the rest of the argument cannot follow.
3 Aquinas' argument that everything needs a cause is simply a viewpoint. Who is to say that everything needs a cause? Just because Aquinas had no evidence of uncaused things does not make such things impossible. If there are uncaused things, then the rest of the argument fails.
4 Similarly, even if everything needs a cause, it is simply a matter of opinion to argue that there must have been a first cause rather than an infinite series of causal regressions without any need for a first cause.

5 Why did such a being need to be God? Or even a being? If this being was uncaused then his argument that there must have been a first cause for this uncaused being has just been contradicted. (And so the argument defeats itself.)

6 Even if there must have been a first cause and that first cause must have been God, this tells us nothing about the nature of this God. It certainly does not make any special case for it being the God in whom Christians believe.

7 Even if this first cause was the God in whom Christians believe, it does not tell us that this God still exists. Perhaps the energy expended in creating the universe caused the death of this God – or perhaps he moved out entirely to a parallel set of universes where he has nothing to do with our universe.

Talk Point

How successfully do you think Aquinas has used the cosmological argument to support belief in the existence of the God he believed in?

3 The cosmological argument from Gottfried Wilhelm Leibniz

Gottfried Wilhelm Leibniz (1646–1716) was a philosopher, scientist and mathematician who was also a religious person. His version of the cosmological argument builds upon and attempts to extend previous versions. In particular, he wanted to get around the need for God – the first cause – to be caused. He produced a line of argument which has come to be understood as based on the 'principle of sufficient reason'. His argument is as follows:

▶ Any fact about the world must have an explanation.
▶ It is a fact that there are contingent things in the universe (things which could just as well have not existed).
▶ So this fact – the existence of contingent things – must have an explanation.
▶ Contingent things cannot ultimately be explained by other contingent things.
▶ So there must be an explanation for contingent things which involves a non-contingent (or necessary) thing (or being).
▶ Therefore there must be a necessary thing (or being).
▶ Contingent beings require to be caused, necessary beings do not.

Strengths of Leibniz's argument

Like Plato and Aquinas, Leibniz used reason and logic to support belief in the existence of God rather than relying on beliefs alone, sacred texts or the teachings of a faith. Leibniz also tried to develop further the element of observable evidence to support the argument – there is evidence to support the existence of things and these things must have had an origin other than themselves. This, he argued, provides sufficient reason to conclude that there is an uncaused being.

Weaknesses of Leibniz's argument

Again, many of the responses apply equally to other forms of the cosmological argument and they raise the following questions:

1 Why should any fact about the universe require an explanation? Perhaps what we observe and experience in the universe is all an illusion.

2 Even if what we observe and experience in the universe is objectively and actually real, why does it need any explanation? Perhaps everything 'just is' – no explanation is required.

3 Why can contingent things not cause/explain other contingent things? Perhaps there has been an infinity of contingent things, each causing the next.

4 If there is a need for a necessary being, why can't the universe itself simply be necessary? And even if there was a necessary being, why does there only need to be one?

5 Even if there was only one necessary being, why does this need to be any particular kind of being?

Those who reject Leibniz's argument would claim that his introduction of the necessary being which needs no cause does not really make his argument any more convincing than any of the others. In fact, it could be argued that reaching any conclusion, perhaps especially one as big as this, requires more than sufficient reason – it requires completely solid and convincing reason.

Talk Point

What do you think about the idea of a 'necessary being'?

4 The Kalam cosmological argument

This argument goes back to the world of medieval Muslim philosophers, such as Al-Ghazali, but some argue that its modern version draws upon the scientific theory of the origins of the universe as the result of a Big Bang. The argument is as follows:

▶ All things which begin have a cause (for nothing can stretch back infinitely).
▶ The universe began and therefore has a cause.
▶ The cause of the universe could only be God.
▶ Therefore God exists.

Strengths of the Kalam argument

Like the others, this argument attempts to provide some scientific backing to the view that nothing can come into existence by itself and applies some objective scientific support to the pure argument. How well it does this is, of course, debatable, since some believe that at the most complex levels of physics there is evidence to support things coming into existence spontaneously without need for a prior cause.

Weaknesses of the Kalam argument

Again, most of the criticisms of the Kalam argument also apply to the other forms of cosmological argument.

1 On what basis is it claimed that all things which begin have a cause? Perhaps the universe is, and always has been, full of uncaused things.
2 Does the argument imply that we must accept God/a divine being as an explanation for the origin of the universe? Why? Does the universe need a cause?
3 The argument implies that God did not begin and therefore did not need a cause. This is a statement of belief, not logic. If God needed no cause, why did anything else?
4 A very big leap of logic is needed to go from saying that the universe needed a cause to saying that this cause must have been God and, in fact, must have been a specific God. Any uncaused cause might be anything.
5 Even if God was the uncaused cause, this does not tell us anything about whether God remains involved in the universe, or exists, or anything else about any of his possible qualities and characteristics.

Do cosmological arguments prove or disprove the existence of God?

Some will argue that cosmological arguments provide a strong case for the requirement for a God and/or God's existence but others will disagree. Some may argue that while the arguments support the philosophical possibility of a God existing, they do little to prove or disprove it in reality. For some people, arguing about first causes is not all that meaningful or productive. Some prefer to start with the universe as it is today and use that to support (or reject) their belief in a creator and support or reject their belief in the existence of God. This argument, known as the teleological argument, or argument from design, is what we will consider next.

Religious arguments, theories and evidence: the teleological argument

As the spaceship approaches the planet, the mystery remains. This planet – known as P-110DJ – has so far avoided discovery by any beings in the universe. How odd then, that now it is about to be seen up close for the first time by a species which only a hundred or so years ago developed enough technology to be accepted into the universal planetary union.

Humans came late onto the universal travel scene, after the discovery of Granitite by the Dundonian environmentalist Wayne Albright. How Albright discovered this substance remains a mystery, but he often exudes a strange glow and has a bad habit of bleeping every time he goes through an airport scanner. Some say he had a close encounter with otherworldly beings not far from Kirriemuir ... No matter. Albrightian Granitite was very soon adopted by the military to power long-distance space travel. In fact, it has the capacity to propel spacecraft at close to the speed of light. Even the aliens were impressed, though Aberdonians ensured that they were kept well away from sources of Granitite.

But back to the spacecraft ... No one has so far penetrated the thick cloud cover of this unnamed planet, but it looks as if the crew of the Starship Broughty might be the first. As they break through the cloud, the surface of the planet comes into view, and all is barren ... at first ...

Captain: Helmsman, can ye sharpen up the view, it's no exactly HD is it?

Helmsman: Aye, just calm yerself, I'm workin' oan it.

Captain: Less o your cheek noo. Just get oan wi it.

Helmsman: Aye aye, right enough. It's clearing up noo. I telt ye tae get the windaes cleaned before we left, didn't I? Right, there it is.

Captain: Well cheers for that at last ... Whit's that?

Helmsman: Whit's whit?

Captain: Thon big thing right afore ye.

Helmsman: Jings. I dinnae really ken.

→

Captain: It looks affy like … naw, it cannae be … It's like a big muckle nose is whit it is … lying in the sand.

Helmsman: I see it but I dinnae believe it … but it must be a thoosand kilometres across … And nae mistake, it's a huge hooter right enough.

Captain: We wis telt that this planet is uninhabited and never has been – naebody's ever lived here – naebody's ever been here …

Helmsman: That's whit we were telt; I'll shoogle [**the universal search engine**] it … Naw, yer dead right – never been inhabited.

Captain: So wher did yon big neb come frae then?

Helmsman: Mibbee it's aye been there.

Captain: Aye right.

Helmsman: Mibbee it has – mibbee the wind and rain and the birlin o the planet just brought it intae bein.

Captain: So aw they forces o physics just came thegither and ended up formin a perfectly sculpted, anatomically exact big human hooter, thoosands o kilometres lang?

Helmsman: Why no … ?

Captain: Right, prepare tae send a message tae the high command at Planetary Union headquarters … 'From SS *Broughty*, Captain Jilly McCormack reportin'. We huv arrived at planet P-110DJ and huv sight of the surface o the planet. We are reportin' the presence of a massive sculpture o an anatomically correct human nose embedded in the planet's surface. We will be goin' in for a closer sniff at it. Will report back efterwards. Cheerio the noo.'

Helmsman: High command has noo been telt … Hope we dinnae get the usual snotty response …

Captain: I dinnae think any o us want to be thinking about snot right the noo …

Talk Point

Does the presence of the giant nose suggest the existence of intelligent life on planet P-110DJ?

The teleological argument

The teleological argument is one which attempts to account for the existence of life, the universe and everything in it as being created by an intelligent designer. It goes beyond the First Cause argument because it is based on the observable universe around us and reaches the conclusion that this level of structure and order in the universe could not have happened by chance but instead is the action of an intelligent designer.

The argument can be summarised as follows:

▸ The universe, and life in it, is ordered and structured. We can observe this directly.
▸ It is highly unlikely that the universe and life in it spontaneously organised itself in this way.
▸ Therefore, something must have provided the structure and organisation for the universe and life in it.
▸ Such a being must be incredibly powerful.
▸ The only such being that could do this is God.
▸ Therefore God must exist.

Why does the teleological argument matter?

For many religious people, the idea of a universe coming together by chance is unacceptable. First it means that no creator God was required and so this is a direct challenge to their belief in God. Second, a universe which has come together by chance might be considered by many religious people as a meaningless and purposeless universe. If everything in life is considered to be the result of combinations of random chance events, then what meaning does our life have? Religious people tend to argue that there is meaning and purpose to it all and that God has 'a plan'. This would be harder to argue if the universe was a chance and random set of happenings.

Talk Point

Do you think that life's meaning might be challenged by the view of the universe as coming together completely randomly?

Paley's watchmaker analogy

Perhaps the best-known version of the teleological argument comes from William Paley (1743–1805) in his book *Natural Theology*, published in 1802. His argument can be summarised as follows:

- Imagine strolling across a field and coming across a stone lying on the ground; I might think that the stone had lain there forever.
- But suppose instead of a stone, I come across a watch. With the watch, I would have to assume that someone had created it and put it there.
- In fact, a watchmaker of great skill must have made the watch. (At the time, watches were mechanical and filled with tiny, delicate machinery which was very intricate and carefully put together.)

Now this led Paley to compare such a watch with the universe:

- Everything in nature works together in very complex ways – just like a watch. So, just as there is a watchmaker, there must also be a maker of all things in nature.
- In nature, however, this complexity is much greater than a watch, and so any maker of nature must also be vastly greater than a maker of a watch.
- The only conclusion which can be drawn is that nature has such a designer and the only possible conclusion is that such a designer matches with our idea of God.

Paley therefore concluded that, in the same way that a watch required a watchmaker, so a universe required a universe-maker. In the same way that it would not be possible for all the components of a watch to come together randomly over time and build themselves into a working watch, equally it would be absurd to think that the universe could come together perfectly by itself with no need for a designing hand.

Paley's watchmaker argument also suggests that just as a watch has been put together for a specific purpose (to indicate the time), so, too, must the universe and all life in it have purpose. A universe coming together all by itself would, for some, suggest that it had no purpose, while a designed universe would be more likely to have some purpose according to the designer's intention in creating it.

Talk Point

What (if any) questions does Paley's argument raise for you?

Contemporary teleological arguments

Modern arguments from design tend to focus more on what has been called the 'Goldilocks effect'. In the same way that Goldilocks eventually found everything that was 'just right' for her, so the universe also often exhibits a Goldilocks effect. For example, if the Earth was just a little closer to or further away from the Sun, then life as we know it might not be possible on Earth. Also, if the proportions of gases in the atmosphere were just a little different, then life on Earth might not be possible. So it seems that the universe is perfectly balanced ('just right') for the development of life. According to contemporary teleological arguments, this fact points to an intelligent designer rather than the blind forces of chance.

Strengths of the teleological argument

Many religious people may accept the teleological argument without much philosophical reflection. They might simply argue that the beauty, power, size, complexity and so on of the universe suggests that it must have been created by an intelligent designer – as well as the fact that everything is 'just right'. So, for them, the universe is evidence of a designer. Who exactly they think this designer was will be linked more closely to other factors – such as their pre-existing beliefs, their culture, their upbringing and so on. Such people will argue that the universe cannot be a random and spontaneous thing which simply formed itself, but that it must have been formed by something even greater than the universe itself. To these people, only gods or God fall into the category of 'greater than the universe', therefore gods/God must exist. This argument is based on logic and belief alone – although some may argue that there is other evidence available in support of an intelligent designer.

Supporters of intelligent design and creation science argue that not only does it make logical sense for there to have been an almighty designer, but that there is evidence to support this view. Intelligent design suggests the following:

▶ Scientifically, it is highly improbable that the universe and life could have formed itself without any intelligent designer planning and orchestrating the process. The laws of probability suggest that the likelihood of everything happening by chance is just too great for it to be true. Many analogies are used – such as the argument that a group of chimpanzees left in a room full of typewriters will eventually come to type the first line of a Shakespeare play. Even with trillions of years, it is argued, this couldn't happen – so what's the likelihood of a universe coming together by chance, no matter how much time is available for it to happen? Therefore laws of mathematical probability make it unlikely that the universe came about by 'chance'.

▶ Intelligent design and creation science supports the concept of irreducible complexity: the idea that physical systems (and living things) require all their parts to be there to contribute to their basic functions. If you take away something from this (and therefore reduce the complexity of the system/thing) then you no longer have the physical system (or living thing). So the universe and life in it only make sense when it is all working together rather than just randomly forming (just as a watch would not work without all of its parts being there and working together to produce watch functionality). Intelligent design cites a number of specific examples of things which only work when all the parts are there and working together efficiently.

▶ Intelligent design also draws upon scientific principles to show that conditions in the universe are just right for the development of life (specifically life on Earth, of course). Intelligent design takes the view that this Goldilocks effect cannot be down to chance, but must be the result of the action of an intelligent designer – creating a universe suitable for life.

Weaknesses of the teleological argument

▶ What appears to be order and structure, no matter how complex, is simply appearance. Just because something looks structured and ordered doesn't mean that it is. Just because something looks designed doesn't mean that it was designed. So the universe may appear designed, but that does not mean it *was* designed.

▶ The universe and life may seem beautiful and well constructed but this is simply us humans projecting our thinking on to it. In fact, the universe is a fairly random place where completely unexpected and really pretty pointless things happen all the time. For example, when a lion kills and eats a baby wildebeest, does that mean that all along 'God's

plan' for that baby wildebeest was that it would have a pretty nasty death in order to become the lion's dinner? Also, many people experience suffering in life because they were 'in the wrong place at the wrong time'. Does this imply that God planned for them to be there at that time to experience whatever it was they went through? The random and cruel nature of existence suggests that if it was designed by an intelligent being then either the design was badly flawed and so the designer was not up to the job or the design is as the designer intended and so we have to question what kind of designer was responsible for it.

- Even if you accept the argument that the universe was designed, its existence doesn't really say much about its designer. Why would it need to be gods/God? Why any particular God? Even if it was designed, this does not prove that the designer is still here, or is still in the same form, or is in the least bit interested in us, and so on. To say that the universe suggests the possibility (or even probability) of an intelligent designer says nothing about that being's existence in reality.

- Many argue that although the probability of the universe and life in it randomly forming itself seems remote, it is actually more likely than we imagine. Laws of probability may well allow for the chimpanzees randomly typing the first line of a Shakespeare play. The numbers involved in the likelihood are incredibly huge, but perhaps not unimaginable. Non-religious people will argue that, given the timescale of the universe, randomly forming life and physical structures are perfectly possible.

- Non-religious people might also argue that the systems and life forms which fill the universe (as far as we know) are those which are a product of the way this universe has developed. If things had randomly happened in a different way in the universe then we would experience different life forms and perhaps different physical principles.

- As to the Goldilocks effect, there is no doubting evidence that shows that certain conditions lead to certain results, but then different conditions lead to different results. For example, if the Earth was just a little closer to the Sun then human life might not have developed, but perhaps other life would have – perhaps nicer life forms, or life which was content just to build great big sculptures of noses in the desert sands …

- As far as irreducible complexity is concerned, many non-religious people argue that systems and organisms do not need to be complete to function usefully. So part of an eye is better than no eye, though not as good as a full eye. In fact, the eye structure does exactly what it needs to do for the organism which makes use of it. By analogy, most other living things have less well-developed brains than humans – but they have brains nonetheless. And while they often can't do things that humans can do because of their 'poorer' brains, they can do exactly what they need to do in their own living environment – and perhaps they do it better than humans could do in that environment even with our developed brains. So even the first tiny bit of Paley's watch would have been a small but useful step towards 'watch-ness'.

Talk Point

Do you think there is good evidence to support or reject the argument from design?

Does the teleological argument prove or disprove the existence of God?

To summarise, supporters of the teleological argument take the view that:

▶ We have a universe which is ordered, structured and works perfectly well for its purpose – a God must have made it that way.

▶ The chances of all of this happening without guidance and purposeful action from a super-intelligent designer seems very small indeed – so there must be a God who is the designer.

▶ Considering the size, complexity and incredible forces at work in the universe, any such designer must be even more powerful than the universe itself.

▶ No matter how you think of this being, the only definition which applies to such a being is what we refer to as 'God'.

▶ Therefore the universe requires the existence of God; therefore God exists.

Personal Reflection

✷ *How important do you think it is to try to prove or disprove the existence of God?*

✷ *Are you convinced by any of the cosmological arguments?*

✷ *Do you think science could ever prove or disprove the existence of God? Should it try to?*

✷ *What do you think of the view that the universe suggests evidence of design?*

✷ *How far does modern science mean that we should no longer base our thinking on only logic and argument?*

✷ *A watch is designed so does that mean a universe has to be designed?*

Apply your learning

Active Learning

1 Create your own artwork and/or graffiti wall which explores possible explanations of 'The meaning of life'.

2 Carry out your own research into people's awareness of and views about cosmological arguments. How much do people know about the arguments and how effective do they think they are?

3 Have a closer look at Big Bang theory. In an extended piece of writing, outline how you think it offers support for cosmological arguments.

4 Continue the dialogue between the Captain, the Helmsman and the Planetary Union headquarters about how far the big nose is evidence of design. (For example, perhaps this planet has many other perfectly natural features which just happen to resemble human anatomy, such as great lakes with what look like giant floating eyeballs in them ...)

5 Turn Paley's watchmaker argument into a manga/action-hero style cartoon, outlining each stage of his argument. If you don't think your art skills are up to this, you could design a poster for a film about Paley's watchmaker argument.

6 Create a display board with cuttings from newspapers/magazines which imply 'good evidence of design' and 'poor evidence of design'.

Investigate

Find out more about:

- ➤ what philosophers mean by *a priori* and *a posteriori* knowledge
- ➤ the lives and backgrounds of Plato, Aquinas, Leibniz and Al-Ghazali. How might their life and times have affected their philosophy?
- ➤ how different religions in the world today respond to cosmological arguments
- ➤ the findings of modern scientific cosmology and how this links or does not link to cosmological arguments
- ➤ views from religions other than Christianity about the teleological argument
- ➤ intelligent design and creation science arguments
- ➤ the life and times of William Paley and how these might have affected his argument
- ➤ examples of a possible Goldilocks effect and challenges to the idea
- ➤ examples of how people look for meaning and pattern (such as 'cold reading' techniques)
- ➤ examples of apparently good and bad design in the universe.

For each of these, report your findings in a manner of your choice. This could be a written report or presentation – in the form of tables, graphs and charts – or as the source of material for a class debate or discussion. You should select a method for your report which is most appropriate for the aspect you are investigating.

Check Your Understanding

1   What reasons might religious people give for wanting the cosmological argument to be true?
2   How might non-religious people respond to your answer to question 1?
3   What different views might be given in answer to the question 'Does it matter how the universe began?'
4   In your own words, describe Plato's cosmological argument.
5   Outline what you think is the most important criticism of Plato's argument.
6   In what important way does Aquinas' argument differ from Plato's?
7   In what ways might Aquinas' argument be challenged?
8   What did Leibniz mean by a 'necessary being'?
9   What (if anything) do you think the Kalam cosmological argument adds to the other arguments?
10 Do scientific findings about the origin of the universe support or reject the cosmological argument?
11 How effective do you think the cosmological argument is in proving or disproving the existence of God?
12 What is the main aim of the teleological argument?
13 In what ways does the teleological argument support/challenge religious belief?
14 Describe Paley's watchmaker argument.
15 What is meant by the 'Goldilocks effect'?
16 In what ways do religious people support the teleological argument using logic/belief alone?
17 What evidence do those who support intelligent design claim to have to support the argument from design?
18 In your view, what are the major strengths and weaknesses of using the argument from design to prove/disprove the existence of God?

Analyse and Evaluate

1   'It is perfectly reasonable, using argument alone, to assume that God created everything.' Discuss.
2   'The cosmological argument provides a very weak argument for the existence of God.' Discuss this claim.
3   'Cosmological arguments provide support for the possibility of God but not for the reality.' Discuss this claim. In your answer you must provide a reasoned and well-structured view.
4   'The universe is evidence for the existence of God.' Discuss this claim.
5   To what extent does the teleological argument support the possibility of a designer but not the actual existence of a creator?
6   'Examples of poor design in the universe challenge the view that it was designed.' Discuss.

Non-religious arguments, theories and evidence

6

The creator bacterium argument

Observe the world around you. Although it's not immediately obvious to you, it is reasonable to assume that the greatest number of living beings on this planet are bacteria. These living things seem to be quite invincible and manage to outsmart every other living creature which has ever attempted to wipe them out. Therefore, by any argument, bacteria are a mighty set of living beings who, it could be argued, rule planet earth.

Now imagine some creator who designed and produced this planet. Would it not be reasonable to assume that this being would make as many things as possible which closely resembled herself/himself/itself?

Therefore, would it not be reasonable to reach the conclusion that any creator of life on Earth must have been a bacterium?

Of course, the counter-argument could be that, as far as we are aware, bacteria do not have the capacity to create living things of incredible complexity, but that's not the point. All bacteria need to do is produce other bacteria.

Therefore, the first great almighty bacterium only had to produce other bacteria, which then developed into the incredible variety of life we have today (with bacteria still top of the heap).

So, it is logical to conclude that the first cause of life on earth was a bacterium and, by analogy, the first cause of everything was a bacterium.

(Profound apologies to all viruses out there.)

Talk Point

How effectively does this argument support the view that any creator must have been a bacterium?

Non-religious perspectives on the existence of God: argument-based

Challenges to the existence of God fall in to two categories: those based on reason, logic and abstract argument – like the bacterium example above – and those based on evidence. In the first category, some might say that arguments for the existence of God contain logical fallacies which mean they are unable to prove the existence of God. This might include, for example, the argument that nothing can come into being without having been caused – except God. This is logically contradictory and so fails as an argument.

Even those arguments which might avoid being logically contradictory do not lead to the conclusion that any creator God/divine being is the God of any specific religious group, or that this being continues to exist, or that this being can, in any way, be something we can communicate with, know about and which has any interest in us. Perhaps, if the arguments are correct and there must be a divine creator, this divine creator might not be something we would like to meet and might not, in any way, match our thinking about what a divine creator is/does, etc.

Logic and argument can only take us so far in our search for conclusions about what is and isn't true. Logic, reason and argument exist in our mind – they provide a process to help us make sense of things – but what happens in our minds does not automatically translate to what happens in reality. For example, imagine convicting someone of a crime because, after thinking through the case very carefully, we reach the conclusion that the person 'must have done it'. We would surely want the decision to send someone to prison to be based on something more concrete than that. Think again about the bacterium argument which opens this chapter …

Non-religious people might well argue that reason alone can call into question the existence of God. They might say that no matter how much thinking you put into it, or how reasonable it seems, argument alone is insufficient to reach the conclusion that there must be a God. In fact, argument might point you in entirely the other direction. This is because you could argue that God is logically impossible (an uncreated being) or that many other factors call into question the existence of God (lack of reliable evidence from those who have seen/heard him; the incompatibility of suffering and evil with the existence of a good God, etc.).

Talk Point

Is argument enough to prove or reject the idea of God?

Non-religious perspectives on the existence of God: evidence-based

While some will continue to debate the logic of the arguments, science continues to seek evidence about the origins of the universe and the extent to which it requires anything which might be considered a cause – and therefore the existence of that cause.

In scientific thinking, something has to be, in principle, *verifiable* (able to be shown to be true) and *falsifiable* (able to be shown to be false). Now, while the physics of the origin of the universe might be verifiable and falsifiable (you can find some information about this in the previous topic – you might not be studying that but have a look anyway), what might have caused the universe is less likely to be verifiable and falsifiable – especially if it is in the form of a divine being of some kind. Science may be able to comment on physical laws and principles which might have led to a self-generating universe but, as yet, science has no 'God test' and so the idea of a divine creator is neither verifiable nor falsifiable.

Currently, scientific thinking takes the view that matter, time and space began at the moment of the Big Bang. So the universe, according to science, had a definite beginning. However, science is not yet able to say categorically that the Big Bang was the first and only beginning of a universe; perhaps 'the' universe has started, lived and died many times before – for all eternity in fact – so although this one had a beginning, all the other universes before it stretch back to infinity. Also, some scientists have proposed the possibility that there are other parallel universes besides ours – so did they have a beginning or have they always been (if, indeed, they exist)? There are different views about what happened before the Big Bang and even if the idea of 'before' the Big Bang means anything – so there's certainly not likely to be any scientific evidence about a divine being/entity/gods/God/demiurge coming soon, or about anything else which might have caused the universe to come into existence.

One interesting debate in science which might be relevant is the possibility that things might come into being spontaneously ('from nothing', in fact). Some scientists argue that it is theoretically possible that matter can appear spontaneously, out of nothing (although there are disagreements about what counts as 'nothing'). If so, then it is perhaps equally possible that the universe might have appeared spontaneously. Others argue that any 'evidence' we have for this is not a true parallel to the beginning of the universe because even if something appeared spontaneously out of nothing right now, something spontaneously appearing here and now is not necessarily the same as something

Talk Point

Is evidence for or against God verifiable and/or falsifiable?

appearing at the beginning of the universe. Some go further and argue that even if some sub-atomic particle or other appears to come into existence spontaneously (and this is not universally agreed), that is still a long way from saying that an entire universe can do the same thing. We are left in something of a difficulty because something coming into being spontaneously at the beginning of the universe may not yet be able to be verified or falsified.

Non-religious (and religious!) people could take the view that there is simply no way to verify or falsify the existence of God since there is no scientific test for God. This means that the existence of God is something which science cannot support or reject with evidence. However, many non-religious people would argue that science is able to provide evidence for a range of things which people sometimes explain by citing the existence of a God. If science provides this kind of explanation for some things, perhaps it will eventually be able to provide evidence which provides an alternative for all things which are currently 'explained' as being evidence for the existence of God.

Scientists have amassed a great deal of evidence which supports both evolution and an origin of the universe without the need for a God, and this evidence, while it doesn't directly disprove the existence of God, indirectly makes God's existence seem less likely.

However, it is possible that this evidence could be challenged in two ways. First, is the evidence sufficient to disprove the existence of God? There may be gaps in the evidence, assumptions about aspects of the evidence and, where the evidence is inconclusive, leaps of logic which are, at the end of the day, based on what 'must be' or 'can't be' rather than what 'is' or 'is not'. Second, no matter how solid the evidence, it still requires to be interpreted and understood. This leaves open the possibility of interpreting the evidence in one way rather than another – perhaps giving more weight to evidence which supports your already existing views rather than challenges them. Let's now have a look at how a non-religious person might respond to both the cosmological and teleological arguments.

Non-religious perspectives on the cosmological argument

Challenges to the cosmological argument (see Chapter 5) begin with the view that the universe and life did not need to be created, but came into existence spontaneously as a result of natural processes. Therefore, there is no need for a creator or intelligent designer of any kind. Non-religious people are likely to take the view that the absence of an intelligent designer does not affect life's meaning: you make your own meaning in life. Also, the idea that the universe has a 'purpose' doesn't really make sense to non-religious people. The universe 'obeys' the blind and morally neutral laws of physics: there is cause and effect. This is just how things are, and there is no need to read into this any idea about meaning in the universe – to do so is meaningless. For many non-religious people, the argument from design falls down in a number of respects expressed nicely for us by David Hume in the eighteenth century.

Hume's response to the cosmological argument

One well-known non-religious argument rejecting the existence of God comes from David Hume (1711–1776). Hume was a Scottish philosopher who responded to the claims of cosmological arguments. His view was as follows:

- If you can accept the idea that God is an uncaused cause, then the universe could have begun without a cause as well. It is no more logical to claim that God is uncaused than that the universe is. In fact, it could be less logical since the universe is clearly here and therefore the fact that it has come into existence can be demonstrated. God, however, is not visible and so there is an extra issue here about proposing the existence of an uncaused being, the proof of which still remains a matter of opinion.

- There is no particular reason to believe that everything needs a cause – so no particular need to believe that the universe does. Just because we might not like the idea of a beginning-less universe doesn't mean there had to be a beginning. Also, why are some religious people very opposed to the idea of the universe having no beginning, but happy with the view that God had no beginning? Of course, religious people will respond that having God create the universe gives it a different level of purpose than if it came into being itself or has always existed. Non-religious people would disagree.

- Even if everything needs a cause, this does not automatically mean that the universe as a whole needs one. It is perfectly reasonable to accept that individual things in the universe need a cause without that necessarily meaning that the universe in its entirety needs one.

- Even if the universe had been caused by a divine being, this tells us nothing about what he/she/it is like – and certainly does not automatically support belief in any particular God. It also does not tell us if this God is still around. Perhaps the God ceased to exist after causing the universe. Perhaps the God *is* the universe. Perhaps the God wants nothing to do with the universe.

Talk Point

What do you think of Hume's argument?

Hume's response to the teleological argument

In his *Dialogues Concerning Natural Religion* (1779), the Scottish philosopher David Hume presented the following criticisms of the teleological argument:

1 **The appearance of design does not necessarily lead to the conclusion that it must have been or was designed.** What Hume is saying here is probably linked to our tendency to try to attach meaning to whatever we encounter. For example, if someone said to you that you had a relative whose name began with 'J' or 'G', your mind would immediately search around for a possible match. You might quickly conclude that the person who said this knows something about you or has psychic powers or something like that. Humans try to make sense of what's around them – so it's no surprise then that we try to make sense of the universe by projecting meaning and purpose on to it and crediting its existence to a designer who has certain qualities which we like (perfectly good, all-powerful, etc.).

2 **If there was a designer, who designed him/her/it?** This is linked to the First Cause argument. If the existence and form of the universe suggests evidence of a designer, then why would the existence and form of a designer not suggest another designer and so on backwards to infinity?

3 **If this designer is the God that those who produced the argument from design believed it to be, then is this God like us?** If so, perhaps he has faults just like us and so perhaps we might doubt the design he has come up with. (For example, did the flood story in the Bible suggest that he had got it wrong with humanity and needed to start all over again?)

4 **Why did supporters of the argument from design always conclude that there must be one designer?** Why not a team of designers?

5 **Perhaps our idea of God needs to be altered.** Perhaps the universe itself is 'God'. It could therefore have made itself or always existed (since supporters of the teleological argument believed that God could have made himself or has always existed). Perhaps, indeed, the laws of physics themselves are God.

6 **Even if the universe was designed by God, this God could be very different from the God that those who produced the teleological argument believed in.**

7 **The universe displays many examples of disorder, chaos and what looks like not very good design.** This contradicts the basis of the teleological argument that the universe and everything in it is perfectly ordered, structured and formed and 'just right'. Some regard this last point as Hume's major criticism. Earlier in this book there is a story of a wasp that lays her eggs inside a living caterpillar. The eggs hatch and the wasp larvae feed on the caterpillar from the inside out, slowly bringing about his death. What evidence is this of perfection in nature or good design? And when we think of the harm people can cause – are humans an example of good design?

Those who reject the teleological argument, including Hume, will do so for many reasons, but to summarise their position:

▶ The universe appears to be designed, but appearing to be designed does not mean it *was* designed.
▶ Even if there was any evidence of design, it need not have been designed by any being or by any particular God, and this being or God may no longer exist. It raises an even bigger question about who might have designed this designer (and so on …).
▶ The universe shows much evidence of poor design which calls into question the existence of any designer.
▶ Taking all of this together, a designer does not need to – and, on the balance of probability, does not – exist.

Non-religious perspectives on the teleological argument

Challenges to the teleological argument (see Chapter 5) based on reasonable argument are as follows:

Although the universe might look ordered and structured, that doesn't mean that this was done by a creator (and any particular kind of creator at that). Also, although we think of nature as ordered and structured it can be random, chaotic and horrible – what kind of God would create a universe like that? Maybe the order and structure we see did come about by chance. And of course, perhaps the universe we have is the one which is the result of the forces at play (non-divine ones) – a different universe is just as possible. Also, given the timescales, the order and structure we see could have developed progressively over time from, for example, a light-sensitive patch on an organism to a fully functioning eye over many millions of years.

Talk Point

How convincing is the non-religious perspective on the teleological argument?

Strengths and weaknesses of non-religious arguments about the existence of God

Strengths

Non-religious people might argue that the key strength of their arguments is that they are, at the end of the day, far more compelling than religious arguments. They might say that most religious arguments tend to either begin with an already existing belief in God or involve a logical fallacy which makes the argument fail (e.g. everything needs a cause, except God). However, non-religious people might suggest that argument alone is insufficient – what is needed is argument coupled with evidence.

Weaknesses

The key weakness perhaps is that an argument is just an argument and can only be taken so far. A non-religious person might think that an argument provides pretty solid logical and philosophical proof that God does not exist, but of course that's not the same as saying it provides actual evidence-based proof that God does not exist. In short, if argument cannot prove the existence of God, then by the same measure, it cannot disprove the existence of God. For this reason, many non-religious people will reach the conclusion that arguments and theories only go so far to support or refute any belief in the existence of (a) God – what is needed is irrefutable physical evidence.

Strengths and weaknesses of non-religious evidence about the existence of God

Strengths

The strength of any evidence is that it is something which can be tested and demonstrated repeatedly. Because it often has a physically observable, experiential quality, we can recognise, gather and assess it. This is more effective than thought alone, which is more likely to lead to conclusions about what must be, rather than what is. Also, evidence-gathering has strict rules and principles as outlined in widely-agreed scientific methods. Non-religious people might argue that evidence is always open to challenge and therefore open to being replaced with a better explanation. This is a key strength of an evidence-based approach which can be flexible and adaptable as we learn more: evidence for or against the existence of God may yet be uncovered – and science would have to accept its findings if it was gathered using scientific method.

Weaknesses

The first weakness is that there is currently no failsafe way to gather evidence to support or reject the existence of a God. God, by definition, is a spiritual entity and as yet science is not able to gather evidence about 'spiritual things' (or even have a common view about what 'spiritual' means). There is currently no scientific test which could provide evidence of whether God exists or not and if evidence for or against the existence of God is absent, then we're back to the problem that 'absence of evidence is not evidence of absence'.

The second weakness is that whatever evidence there might be to support the view that God does not exist remains a matter of interpretation. There is pretty strong evidence for Big Bang and evolutionary theories, but this does not automatically rule out the possibility of a God being behind it all. There is no way to gather information to support or reject that idea but concluding that there is no God because there is evidence for something else (Big Bang and evolution) is a little tricky.

Talk Point

Is it ever going to be possible to gather evidence for the existence of God?

Personal Reflection

* *Do you think religious or non-religious arguments about the existence of God best answer the question about God's existence?*
* *Non-religious people argue that life has a perfectly good meaning without the need for a God. What do you think?*
* *What do you think of the argument that evidence showing chaos and disorder in the universe proves there is no creator God?*

Apply your learning

Active Learning

1. Script a dialogue based on the 'creator bacterium' argument at the start of this chapter. You could try to do this in Scots or Doric or in rhyme.
2. Create a newspaper front page where the headline is 'Proof that God does not exist'. What do you think would be the possible implications of this for human society, if any?
3. Create your own web page about David Hume's arguments against the existence of God.
4. Create your own 'ABC' poem using what you have learned about religious and non-religious arguments, theories and evidence about the existence of God. (For an extra challenge you could try to make it rhyme.) For example, 'A is for Atheist who thinks there's no God; B is for Bible, which says that's quite odd …'

Investigate

Find out more about:

➤ scientific method and how scientists find 'proof'
➤ what Karl Popper said about verification and falsification
➤ the 'God Helmet' and whether this provides evidence for or against God
➤ the difference between quantitative and qualitative data and how scientists arrive at both
➤ the evidence a non-religious person might give for stating that there is no God
➤ responses to non-religious views about the existence of God across different religions.

For each of these, report your findings in a manner of your choice. This could be a written report or presentation – in the form of tables, graphs and charts – or as the source of material for a class debate or discussion. You should select a method for your report which is most appropriate for the aspect you are investigating.

Check Your Understanding

1 What 'logical fallacies' do non-religious people challenge in religious arguments for the existence of God?
2 Do you agree that 'logic and reasoning can only take us so far in our search for conclusions of what is and isn't true'?
3 What is meant by verifiable and falsifiable?
4 Could a test for the existence of God be devised?
5 Why might someone argue that gaps in the evidence to disprove the existence of God mean the evidence must be rejected?
6 How might someone who disagrees with the response to the previous question respond?
7 Explain two of Hume's arguments rejecting religious views about the cosmological argument. What do you think of Hume's responses?
8 What do you think are the strongest and weakest arguments put forward by Hume in response to the teleological argument?
9 Describe one strength and one weakness of a non-religious argument about the existence of God.
10 What are the strengths and weaknesses of evidence against the existence of God from a non-religious perspective?
11 Do you think religious or non-religious arguments are the most successful arguments about the existence of God? What leads you to this conclusion?
12 Do you think there is, or could ever be, conclusive proof that God exists?

Analyse and Evaluate

1 'God can neither be proved nor disproved, therefore there is no point in talking about God.' Discuss this claim.
2 To what extent are the cosmological and teleological arguments lacking in evidence?
3 'Non-religious arguments, theories and evidence provide strong support for the view that God does not exist.' Discuss.
4 'Hume's views are from the early eighteenth century, so we shouldn't take them into account in the twenty-first century'. What do you think?

Can either religious or non-religious explanations provide conclusive proof about the existence of God?

Method

Mix all of the above together carefully, adding each ingredient as it becomes necessary. Once ready, enjoy a life of meaning and purpose.

Method

Combine the ingredients as required. Once ready, enjoy a life of meaning and purpose.

Does it matter whether God exists or not?

For many people, this is one of the most fundamental big questions of all. Is there a God? What is this God like? What does this God's existence – or lack of existence – mean for our lives? There are a variety of possible views:

1   For many, this is an important question because it says a great deal about how we should live our lives, and what might be the meaning and purpose of life. If there is a God, then perhaps we should examine our lives very carefully and live them as if they matter to God. If God created everything then he obviously intended there to be some kind of relationship between him and his creation, and it is therefore our job to live accordingly. For non-religious people there is no need of a God to give our lives meaning and purpose – that can be achieved without God. In fact, for non-religious people, whether God exists or not is irrelevant to our lives.

2 Religious people are likely to argue that our moral actions will be affected by the existence of God – since how we live our lives might result in reward and/or punishment by God. This is not the only reason why most religious people behave morally, but it is an important motivation for many. Non-religious people might respond that we should live good moral lives regardless of the existence of any God. Our motivation to behave morally should come from within – not be imposed externally by some divine being.

3 Many religious people also argue that God has 'a plan' for each of us – and that we should live our lives in accordance with that plan. Non-religious people argue that because there is no God, there can be no plan and it is up to us to make decisions in life. (Besides, they might add, if God has a plan why does he not share it with us?)

4 For some religious people believing in God gives them strength, courage and hope. They believe ultimately that God will look after them and this gives them comfort – especially when life is hard. Non-religious people might argue that we are projecting our need here and creating a universal parent figure to care for us – this might well be comforting but it is also a delusion. They would add that personal strength, courage and hope do not need to rely on the existence of a God.

5 For many religious people, believing in God helps them cope with one of life's biggest concerns – that one day we will die. Belief in God helps them because they believe death is not the end. (Buddhists have no God but also believe that death is not the end.) Non-religious people are likely to argue that we can cope with death without having to believe in a God. Death is, indeed, the end, but our memory lives on in others and how we live the one life that we have is more important than anything that happens after it.

Talk Point

How would you answer the question: Does belief in God matter?

Religious and non-religious explanations: opposing or complementary?

The issues surrounding the existence of God can be approached from a religious perspective or from a non-religious perspective or from some combination of the two. Within and between each perspective there can be agreement, disagreement and, perhaps, compatibility – though this isn't always possible. It's fair to say that there is likely to be greater disagreement about the existence of God between religious and non-religious perspectives than between different religious perspectives, though, of course, this won't always be the case.

The options in answer to the question which this chapter deals with are:

▶ There is no possible way to provide conclusive proof about the existence of God at this moment in time and there never will be.

▶ There is no possible way to provide conclusive proof about the existence of God at this moment in time but at some point there might be.

▶ While 'conclusive proof' will remain difficult to achieve, some degree of proof is or might be possible to obtain – perhaps there is, or will be, 'sufficient proof'.

▶ Religious arguments, theories and evidence provide conclusive proof that God exists.

▶ Non-religious arguments, theories and evidence provide conclusive proof that God does not exist.

It is important to be aware, however, that the debate about conclusive proof is not just between religious and non-religious perspectives – it can be within them too. This chapter will focus on the cosmological and teleological arguments and deal with these from a Judaeo-Christian point of view, as well as from non-religious perspectives.

Religious explanations

For some, religion involves believing without seeing or, at least, believing without the need for evidence to confirm the truth of the religion. This doesn't mean that religious people completely ignore evidence – in fact, many religious people think that there is plenty of evidence to back up their beliefs. For example, while most would not claim to have seen God, many religious people argue that their feeling of his presence or his actions in the world are evidence enough of his existence. Some religious people do claim to have had direct experience of God and when this happens they accept as a matter of faith their particular interpretation of what they have experienced. For many, religion is a perfectly reasonable way to approach life. Some challenge those who live according to religious beliefs, arguing that it is not enough just to believe something – you need to have evidence for what you believe. And they might argue that living by faith means you can never be shown to be wrong because you do not allow contradictory evidence to challenge your faith. Religious people might disagree and say that people who live by faith might allow evidence to challenge some aspects of their faith but not their entire faith perspective.

Explanations across religions

Most religions have a belief in some kind of deity – though they often have very different views about the qualities of this deity. Buddhism does not believe in a deity, though in some branches of the religion there is a belief in semi-divine beings. And while most religions involve belief in a deity, there might be very different perspectives on any evidence or argument which might support the existence of that deity. For example, monotheistic religions would be likely to accept both the cosmological argument and the teleological argument, because of their belief in a divine creator. However, in Hindu belief there is a more cyclical understanding of the beginning of things and in Buddhism the absence of a divine figure means there is no need for a creator. There are different views across religions and so it is difficult to speak of one religious explanation. What is more, the importance given to using argument to support belief in God varies significantly across religions.

Talk Point

Should religious people disagree with each other?

Explanations within religions

Even within religions there can be disagreement about the cosmological and teleological arguments. Some within a religion might argue that these are no more than arguments and not necessary to support faith – in fact, they might show a lack of faith through the need to find 'evidence' for the truth of the faith (through argument or demonstrable evidence). Even where religious people accept both arguments, there can still be disagreement about aspects of them – for example, while some might point to the 'beauty' of the natural world as evidence for God, others might equally highlight the 'cruelty' of the natural world as a way of calling into question a particular interpretation of God.

Non-religious explanations

In the case of the existence of God and arguments which might support that, there is likely to be complete agreement between non-religious people, since not believing in any kind of deity is part of what defines being non-religious. Non-religious people may discuss and debate the cosmological and teleological arguments as a matter of philosophy, but since their perspective is based on the absence of belief in God, the debate is likely to be little more than academic. Of course, there may be some level of discussion between non-religious people who are atheists and those who are agnostic but this will be different from the debates concerning the cosmological and teleological arguments which take place within and between religions.

Religious and non-religious perspectives

There could be some agreement about some aspects of the arguments – for example, that the universe requires a point of beginning – but the very definition of religious and non-religious means there will be no agreement on the general conclusions of the arguments.

The cosmological argument

Non-religious responses

The cosmological argument is wrong

- The argument is logically contradictory – you cannot claim that everything needs a cause except God.
- If God can be infinite then so, too, can the universe be infinite.
- It does not follow that even if a first cause was required that this cause must have been any specific God.
- Even if a first cause was required and it was a specific God, it does not follow that this God still exists.
- Even if a first cause was required, this says nothing about any characteristic of this first cause.

The cosmological argument is right

Similarly, the cosmological argument can be accepted as a logical and reasonable set of premises which lead to a logical conclusion – so the premises and conclusions of the argument might be *understood* by a non-religious person, but not *accepted*. This is not to say that non-religious people will accept this as proof of the existence of gods/God or any kind of deity, but simply that the argument supports the view that a first cause is logically necessary. Any non-religious person convinced by the cosmological argument would be likely to take the view that the universe caused itself.

Religious responses

The cosmological argument is wrong

While a religious person from a monotheistic faith is likely to accept the First Cause argument, they could equally reject it based on a rational consideration of the argument and conclude that it is ineffective. In doing so they would simply accept one or more of the arguments in the earlier list. Of course, this does not mean that they reject God as the creator, but that they simply reject the logic of this argument. Their belief in God is a matter of faith, drawing upon the scriptures and teachings of their faith. It is also important to point out that some religions – especially those which do not involve belief in any divine being – can take the view that the universe came about without any need for divine intervention – and/or that it has always existed. Buddhists, for example, could reject the cosmological argument in this way.

The cosmological argument is right

A religious person could easily accept all the premises of the argument, and conclude that it supports their belief in God. However, it is likely that their belief in God will rest on far more than simply one or more philosophical arguments. For example, a religious person might argue that the cosmological argument is right because their scriptures tell them that God created everything.

Are religious and non-religious views compatible?

As you can see, it is possible that religious and non-religious people could accept the cosmological argument without that meaning they accept the consequences in the same way. Similarly, both groups could reject the argument but nevertheless have different reasons for believing or not believing in God. Finally, many religious people will believe in God, and their belief will be completely independent of the cosmological argument, just as many non-religious people will not believe in God and their position will be unrelated to the cosmological argument. So, of course, the answer to this is that some think religious and non-religious views are compatible while others disagree!

The teleological argument

Non-religious responses

The teleological argument is wrong

It is possible to reject the premises and therefore conclusions of the teleological argument based solely on argument:

- The appearance of design does not mean something is designed.
- Even if design is evident, this doesn't automatically require any specific divine being as designer.
- If a divine being did design the universe, the design of the designer still requires to be explained.
- The flawed design of the universe suggests either lack of design or a flawed designer.
- The idea that the universe was designed for a purpose is at odds with its apparent randomness.

The teleological argument is right

Someone could accept all the premises and therefore conclusions of the teleological argument based solely on logic and argument. However, this does not need to mean that the person accepts the continued existence of any designer and/or that any designer might have any specific characteristics and qualities. In fact, perhaps the actions of natural laws brought about the universe in a way which gives the appearance of it being designed – so a 'designer' is necessary, but such a designer is simply the neutral forces of nature and laws of physics.

Religious responses

The teleological argument is wrong

Based on faith, someone could reject the premises and conclusions of the teleological argument in exactly the same way as someone would do based solely on reason. This does not mean that a religious person rejects the existence of an intelligent designer, just that this designer's existence does not rest on argument but on the scriptures and teachings of their faith as well as their own experience of this designer. Believing in a designer may be an emotional response to nature rather than one based on logic and argument. Again, there could be disagreement within and between religions about the status given to, for example, the teleological argument, leading to conclusions not about whether it is right or wrong, but about whether it is relevant or not.

The teleological argument is right

A religious person might accept the teleological argument, especially as it matches up with their experience of the universe as ordered and structured and – perhaps, more importantly – because it matches up with their pre-existing belief which is based on more than argument. This might be the scriptures/teachings of their faith, or their own experience of a designer God. In short, they might take the view that the teleological argument is sound philosophical support for something which is true anyway.

Are religious and non-religious views compatible?

In practice, it is perfectly possible for someone to reject the teleological argument while still retaining their faith in the existence of a God. For religious people, belief in God is stimulated and motivated by a range of factors, of which argument is only one, and many religious people prefer such 'emotional' commitment rather than a commitment based on philosophical argument. Of course, in general, those from monotheistic faiths will accept the design argument because their scriptures teach that God created everything and their experience of the beauty and order of the universe will tend to convince them of this. Apparent flaws in the design of the universe will not be ignored, but responded to with trust that God knows what he is doing. There is likely to be little compatibility between religious and non-religious perspectives – they might agree that order and structure in nature requires some kind of 'governing principle', but that's a very long way from saying that any such 'governing principle' might be a divine being.

So, yet again, the compatibility of religious and non-religious views depends on how you approach this. Like many aspects of this course where two perspectives are being considered (bearing in mind that each 'perspective' will have a number of views within it), there are three possibilities: religious and non-religious views are completely incompatible; religious and non-religious views are completely compatible; religious and non-religious views can be compatible, but only to an extent.

Talk Point

Should religious people use argument and logic to support their beliefs?

Personal Reflection

* *Is it reasonable to accept the cosmological/teleological argument?*
* *Do you think everything in life can be understood logically?*
* *Do only religious people have faith?*

Apply your learning

Active Learning

1 Design and produce an academic poster which outlines religious and non-religious responses to the teleological or cosmological argument.
2 Create a piece of artwork or collage entitled 'Does God exist?'
3 Write an imaginative story entitled 'The day the cosmological argument was proved'.
4 Create a questionnaire about one or more of the issues in this topic and display your findings in the form of graphs, tables, etc.

Investigate

Find out more about:

➤ the Genesis story in the Jewish/Christian scriptures
➤ non-monotheistic views about the cosmological and teleological arguments
➤ different views within religions about the cosmological and teleological arguments
➤ support/rejection for the cosmological and teleological arguments from non-religious perspectives.

For each of these, report your findings in a manner of your choice. This could be a written report or presentation – in the form of tables, graphs and charts – or as the source of material for a class debate or discussion. You should select a method for your report which is most appropriate for the aspect you are investigating.

Check Your Understanding

1 In what ways might religious people disagree about the cosmological argument?
2 Could religious and non-religious people agree about any aspect(s) of the cosmological argument?
3 Would all non-religious people agree that the teleological argument is wrong?
4 In what ways does the existence of God matter to many people?
5 Do you think that believing in God helps people in their life or causes them difficulty?
6 What might a religious person mean by 'God's plan'?
7 What difficulties might the idea of God 'having a plan' present for religious and non-religious people?
8 Why might the teleological argument be a reason to reject belief in God?
9 How might the cosmological argument be defended by a religious person?
10 Do the cosmological and teleological arguments make the existence of God more or less likely (or not affect it)?
11 How might a Buddhist respond to the cosmological/teleological arguments?
12 In your view, is the cosmological or teleological argument stronger support for the existence of God?

Analyse and Evaluate

1 'Religious and non-religious people will never reach compatibility about the cosmological argument.' Discuss.
2 'There is no reasonable argument for the existence of God.' Discuss this claim.
3 Analyse the view that argument alone can prove or disprove the existence of God.
4 'Religious people should require no arguments for their belief that God created everything.' Discuss.

THE PROBLEM
OF SUFFERING
AND EVIL

Is God responsible?

8

The Celestial Bugle

www.celestialbugle.com   THE WORLD'S FAVOURITE NEWSPAPER   - since creation -

GOD APPEARS AND TAKES AWAY ALL ILLNESS

Reports are coming in from around the world of all forms of illness suddenly disappearing following the shock appearance of God in Inverness early this morning. As the world woke to the news that the question 'Does God exist?' is no longer a question, God himself said little other than that he had 'listened' and had 'decided to put an end to speculation about my existence and respond to a question humanity has been asking since the beginning'.

Theologians around the world have been astounded by his appearance, with many now facing new questions over their continued employment. One university spokesperson said: 'Clearly we will now have to review many of our appointments across the University since the reason for their work no longer applies.'

Asked why he had decided to remove all illness first, God apparently replied: 'That's what humanity wanted most of all, so it has been done.' Hospitals are emptying fast, and doctors' surgeries are eerily quiet. A spokesperson for the British Medical Association is reported as saying: 'Doctors will now be a thing of the past – a great many people will have to find alternative careers.'

The world's stock markets reacted nervously to God's appearance – with many seeing huge drops in share prices and a growing sense of panic about the stability of the world's financial systems. One financial expert commented: 'The world's stock markets rely on uncertainty. Now there is certainty, this cannot be a good thing for share prices – for example, the insurance industry will be badly hit by the fact that no one will need to be insured against becoming ill. No good can come of it all.' A spokesperson for the Scottish Government said: 'While, of course, we welcome the news that there will be no more illness, we will now be carefully reviewing our housing and pensions provision since we expect that there will be a significant increase in population.'

Meanwhile, there have been some angry responses from farming communities worried about their ability to cater for the food needs of a larger population – the result of the lack of illness. A spokesperson for the farming community stated: 'We're already having trouble meeting the food needs of our current population – I can't see how we can feed even more.'

There is further speculation that God may also remove all possible sources of evil in the world. This will have significant implications for many people in society, including the police and emergency services, lawyers and a range of other industries and services. After initial joy at God's announcement, some have speculated that the end result of God's purge on all things evil will have effects on all of us. A well-known philosopher has stated: 'The logical end result of all this has to be taking away my right to choose – because if I want to commit an evil act I must now not be able to do so. In fact, I must not be able to think it, since perhaps thinking evil is, in itself, evil. So how might God put an end to this? The answer, of course, can only be that he will put an end to me.'

Leaders around the world are struggling to come to terms with the unfolding events. However, one world leader – who wished to remain anonymous – commented: 'Of course we welcome today's news about illness, and would wish to express our appreciation of God's act. However, we live in a democracy, and no one has the right to rule unless elected by the people.'

What God will do next remains a matter for speculation around the world, but sources close to God say that he has some important issues to address, and that removing illness is only the first one. One source said: 'For as long as humanity has been around it has wanted God to put an end to suffering and evil. Now that this has happened it remains to be seen if humanity understands the full implications of this action.' Another source close to God put it more bluntly: 'Be careful what you wish for.'

Talk Point

Would a world without illness be desirable?

What is suffering?

Suffering is a term which has many different meanings but, in general, it can be thought of as something real or imagined which has the potential to, or does, cause harm. Like many such concepts, suffering can be something which we all experience in similar ways – for example, when you break your arm, the pain you suffer is very similar to the pain anyone else suffers (except for people who experience psychological states where pain experience is absent or different, such as in analgesia). Alternatively, a situation which causes suffering for one person may lead to a different emotion for someone else. Think about the experience of two people running a marathon – one may be suffering and one may be enjoying the experience!

Perhaps we should think of suffering on a sliding scale for each individual – from hardly noticeable to extremely severe. Where your experience of suffering lies on the scale may be unique to you. Four types of suffering can be identified: physical, mental, emotional and spiritual.

▶ **Physical** This can be anything from a slight ache to severe debilitating pain. Physical suffering may be the result of accident, disease and illness, or other internal and external factors which affect you physically in negative ways. Essentially, your senses experience something they don't like and feed back this experience to your brain, where it is processed. Physical suffering can be short and sharp or long and drawn out, and may itself lead to other kinds of suffering.

▶ **Mental** This is where you experience negative mental states and/or mood. Again, this can vary from, for example, feeling slightly down or nervous about something to long-term and severe depression or anxiety. The causes of mental suffering are many and varied and can be linked to physical and environmental factors, illness, genetic conditions and personality type, among other things.

▶ **Emotional** This is similar to mental suffering but can also be, for some people, quite physical. Emotional suffering can have many of the same causes as physical and mental suffering, and is likely to lead to changes in your mood and outlook, and so, perhaps, your behaviour.

▶ **Spiritual** For some, this is a sense of deep mental/emotional suffering which they would define as spiritual. It could, for example, be linked to doubts about belief, or loss, or many other factors. Some might argue that what is termed 'spiritual suffering' is just a part of mental/emotional suffering.

In all situations where suffering is present or possible, it's important to note that it can be because of the presence of something or equally the absence of something. For example, being around someone you don't like might cause suffering, and missing someone you do like can cause suffering too. Suffering can be caused internally – by you, your body or your response to something – or externally – by something outside of you, such as an earthquake. Some would disagree with this and argue that all suffering comes from within, since it is about your response to suffering, while others disagree – but more of that later.

What is evil?

In answer to this question you could simply say 'anything bad' – but what is bad for one person might not be bad for another. Some think of evil as a 'thing' – on occasion giving it a name and even a body. Others think of evil as an idea. Some will use the terms 'evil' and 'suffering' interchangeably – evil might be considered a cause of suffering, while suffering might be considered something evil.

▶ **A force** Some believe that evil is a force – a bit like the 'dark side' in *Star Wars*. This force is out there, but it can also get into individuals, causing them to think and do evil things. It might be thought of as a kind of negative energy. For some, this force has a name and a set of characteristics: evil is personified. Religious people through the ages have called this being Satan, Shaytan, Lucifer, Diabolos, the Devil, Mara and so on, and cite this being (and his/its helpers, such as demons) as the cause of evil. In all these cases the evil has a direct counterpart which is the opposite of evil. Some think of these two forces as equally balanced, while others argue that their (good) deity is always in charge and for some unknown reason permits a certain amount of evil.

▶ **A concept** Some do not think of evil as a physical entity in any way. They prefer to think of it as an idea or a concept. There are likely to be varying viewpoints about the origins and consequences of the existence of this negative concept. Some would also add that evil is not actually a thing in itself but is the absence of good.

▶ **Actions** For some, evil is an action: it is something that we do or something that is done to us. This is a difficult one, because it links to motivation, intention and other factors. For example, causing the death of your best friend in a fight would be considered evil, but people might think differently about causing the death of your best friend in a road accident. Also, thinking about doing something evil might be different from actually doing it – though some might even argue that evil thoughts are just as bad as evil actions.

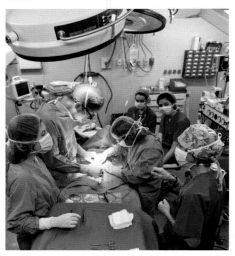

▶ **Consequences, human and natural** Some think that what we call or describe as evil has a range of causes and that the best way to think of evil is as something which is the result of a range of other things. For example, someone chopping off your leg might be considered evil – unless, of course, it is a surgeon who is trying to save your life. Evil is therefore what we experience, and perhaps our interpretation of that experience, and it is completely morally neutral.

When thinking about evil it is also important to consider the distinction between natural evil and human evil. Natural evil is evil which is the result of natural forces (such as a flood or an earthquake), while human evil is that caused by humans.

Suffering and evil: arguments supporting the view that God is responsible

Suffering and evil clearly exist. They harm people and make our world a less pleasant place than it otherwise could be. No one can deny that suffering and evil are realities, and that there has probably never been a being on Earth who has not experienced suffering and/or evil at some point in their existence. At the same time, many people believe in a God or gods and maintain that they have certain qualities. However, it seems that the existence of suffering and evil presents a challenge to God or gods – perhaps because the qualities attributed to these beings are at odds with the existence of suffering and evil. For many, the conclusion reached might be as follows:

▶ The qualities we attribute to this divine being(s) are inaccurate.

▶ This divine being(s) does not exist.

Some would say that the key argument in support of the view that God is responsible for suffering and evil lies with the three main qualities attributed to God. If God is, as monotheists tend to believe, omnipotent (all-powerful), omniscient (all-knowing) and perfectly good, then he is responsible because his omnipotence means he could bring an end to suffering and evil right away, his omniscience means that he knows all about suffering and evil and how to bring it to an end, and his perfect goodness would surely mean that he would want to bring an end to suffering and evil. Despite these qualities, suffering and evil still exist so the fact that God does not seem to be able to or want to do anything about them means that he must be considered responsible for them. In fact, some would say that there are two ways of looking at this – the first is that God causes evil and the second that he doesn't cause it, just permits it. Either way, this wouldn't fit with his key qualities. Let's have a closer look at this key argument.

Monotheistic faiths

Monotheistic faiths consider there to be one supreme God and one alone. There are no other Gods or gods. Christianity gives this God three 'persons' – Father, Son and Holy Spirit – though regards God as 'three in one'. For monotheists, there is a variety of explanations for the nature of God, and many names for God which outline his qualities, such as the 99 names for Allah in Islam. We will focus here on a specifically Christian view of God and a set of qualities for God – omnipotence, omniscience and perfect goodness – which Christian theology has generally accepted throughout the ages. The key question is – can God be these three things while suffering and evil exist?

The challenge to omnipotence

Omnipotence means being all-powerful and is the idea that God is without limits to his power. He can do anything he chooses to do. The challenge presented by suffering and evil is therefore: if God is all powerful and can do anything he chooses, why does he appear to do nothing about suffering and evil? Either he chooses to do nothing and we just have to suffer – which seems wrong – or he can do nothing about it – which means he is not all-powerful. If he is not all-powerful, then in what way can we think of him as God? Surely an all-powerful being would remove suffering and evil. That he appears to do nothing perhaps calls into question his very existence.

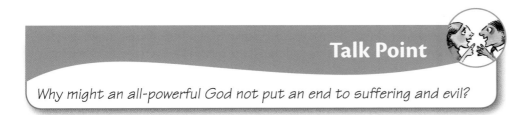

Talk Point

Why might an all-powerful God not put an end to suffering and evil?

Monotheistic perspective and responses

It is possible that some monotheists might consider the three qualities attributed to God as man-made qualities. Just because God has been defined in these ways does not necessarily mean that he *has* these qualities. If we do not accept that he has these qualities then there is no issue in the first place (and this is sometimes the approach taken in non-monotheistic faiths). However, within Christianity, it is arguable that most Christians would accept that God has these three qualities and therefore there is a case to answer.

▶ God gave humans free will and so they might act in evil ways which cause suffering. God cannot give free will and then take it away again. This is his gift to us, but unfortunately it comes at a price – the existence of suffering and evil. God could take away suffering and evil, but he would then have to take away our free will as well, which would make us God's robots. Suffering and evil are an unavoidable fact of our free will. God has the power to remove suffering and evil, but to do so would mean removing our freedom and he chooses not to do so. A non-religious person might question why freedom is more important than taking away suffering, or ask why God doesn't give us the illusion of freedom while preventing us making decisions which could result in real suffering and evil. This might not be 'real' freedom, but perhaps it would be better than having to put up with suffering and evil.

▶ God made a universe with certain physical properties and laws. His omnipotence means he could change these laws completely or intervene at any time to avoid them causing harm. (Some religious people think he does this in the form of miracles.) However, this would be an odd use of his omnipotence, since what would have been the point in making the laws in the first place? If natural laws sometimes led to harm but other times didn't, the result would be a difficult universe in which to live since it would be very unpredictable. Again, a non-religious person might question why an omnipotent God didn't design a universe with perfectly predictable laws which do not result in suffering and evil.

Talk Point

Would God have the power to do something logically contradictory?

The challenge to omniscience

Omniscience is the idea that God is all-knowing. He knows past, present and future, and everything which has and will ever happen. If he is all-knowing, presumably he has a solution for suffering and evil – so why not put this into action? And, if he does know everything, in what way are we really free? If all our choices in life are already known, are they really our choices to make?

Monotheistic perspective and responses

▶ Yes, God knows everything, but that doesn't harm our freedom. If I give you a choice between chocolate and vanilla ice cream I might know, based on my knowledge of your tastes, which one you will choose. But you are still *free* to make your choice.

▶ It would make little sense for God to intervene every time he knows someone is going to make a bad decision – because (perhaps) then they would not be free to do so. There is also a logical problem here. If God knows what any decision will be and intervenes to change it, then he has changed the future by this intervention, and should have known about this in the first place. Therefore he should have known that he would intervene and change your choice, leading to a different consequence! A non-religious person might argue that this logically contradictory state of affairs means that omniscience is a very difficult concept to accept. It may also call into question belief in miracles, where God seems to exercise his omniscience and omnipotence in some cases but not in others. Why is this?

▶ Some monotheists might get around this problem by arguing that omniscience means knowing every possibility, rather than every actuality. God knows all the possible options open to a person when making a choice – but they are still free to make the choice. So the fact that they choose an evil act is not God's responsibility; it is theirs. Also, natural forces can lead to a variety of consequences which God can foresee, but that does not necessarily mean he should intervene to change anything. A non-religious person might argue that while an omniscient God might not want to affect our freedom, why does he not intervene to prevent natural disasters without us having to know about them? In this way he would reduce the amount of suffering and evil in the world, without having any impact on our freedom.

The challenge to God's perfect goodness

The final quality usually attributed to God is that he is perfectly good (also known as omnibenevolent). This means that he is incapable of doing anything bad or wrong, and at all times – and in all situations – acts in good ways. The challenge presented by suffering and evil is therefore: if God is perfectly good, why does he allow suffering and evil to take place when he could bring them to an end? If he chooses to allow suffering and evil then he is, in part, responsible for them. This is not the action of a perfectly good being, therefore he is either not perfectly good or does not exist.

Monotheistic perspective and responses

- God is perfectly good but, for the reasons outlined in relation to his omnipotence and omniscience, he does not bring an end to suffering and evil because this would also bring an end to free will and mean that the natural laws of the universe were rather pointless.
- Some monotheists might argue that 'goodness' needs to be carefully defined. If a parent gives a child a row for wandering off in a shopping centre it might not be thought of as 'good'. But it is ultimately for a good purpose – so is it good or not? Monotheists might argue that God sometimes behaves in ways (or allows things to happen) which do not appear to be good but are so in reality. They have a greater purpose, of which we might not be aware. The child on the receiving end of the row may just think their parent is being nasty when, in fact, they are being kind – since the parent is protecting the child in the future. Perhaps God acts this way when he engages in acts of justice, or perhaps there is some long-term benefit to what appears as suffering and evil. A non-religious person might consider this to be a weak argument. Why does God need to do or allow 'bad' things in order to safeguard us or prevent even worse things from happening? We are not like children who have been left to our own devices – we are intelligent, thinking beings. Why does God need to mother us in this way?

- There are occasions where God seems to have done some rather unpleasant things – such as kill many Egyptians in the Exodus story. There are also occasions where he seems to have allowed some very bad things to happen throughout history, even to his faithful followers. These events seem inconsistent with the idea that God is perfectly good. Monotheists might argue that all this is to be accepted as a matter of faith, while non-religious people might say that this is simply faith ignoring the evidence because that evidence is not convenient.

Talk Point

Does the existence of suffering and evil challenge the existence of a perfectly good God?

Non-monotheistic faiths

The existence of suffering and evil may also present problems for non-monotheistic faiths. Believing in any kind of deity or purpose in life usually implies that things are better when you believe in this way. However, the fact that believers and non-believers seem to suffer the effects of suffering and evil in much the same way raises the question of the benefit of belief in the first place. Why follow a religion or accept its teachings if you still have to suffer the same fate as everyone else? Some non-monotheistic religions nevertheless believe in divine beings. Some regard them as many beings, while others might not really be non-monotheistic at all, since they regard them all as aspects of one divine being. There might be many qualities attributed to divine beings and the existence of evil might challenge their supposed power and/or their very existence. In some religions, these divine beings might be ascribed positive and negative qualities which accounts for evil – but some kind of eternal battle between the 'good gods' and the 'evil gods' raises many significant questions for non-monotheists.

Some non-monotheist faiths are, in fact, atheistic religions – without any belief in a God or gods. For these faiths, the existence of evil is a challenge because it is a potential barrier to their religious life and belief (though Buddhists could argue that the existence of suffering and evil provides the rationale for the faith). Its apparent randomness calls into question the relationship between cause and effect because even those who live carefully (according to the teachings of their religion) still suffer just like everyone else. Perhaps this calls into question ideas like kammic consequences and so on. (In fact, it might add weight to this belief if you consider that these individuals are experiencing the results of their accumulated bad kamma.)

Talk Point

Do you think suffering and evil are illusions?

Non-religious perspectives and responses

There are many reasons why someone follows a religion – far too complex to go into here. How do non-monotheistic faiths respond to the problem of suffering and evil?

- Some take the view that suffering and evil are illusions. There is no such thing as evil; just cause and effect. What is considered evil is just one interpretation that we apply to something rather than another. In some respects, Buddhism treats suffering and evil in this way. They are, like all other experiences and emotions, illusions. Clinging on to the reality of these illusions is the cause of the harm, not the experience/emotion itself. The key is to detach ourselves from this false reality, appreciate that nothing ever stays the same, and not allow our experiences to cause us harm. Non-religious people might argue that evil, pain and suffering are real – not illusions – and that detaching ourselves from their real effects is easier said than done.

- Of course, some non-monotheistic religions respond to suffering and evil by claiming that they are the natural causes and effects of natural laws and, for example, the kammic consequences of actions. In Buddhism, the existence of suffering and evil does not challenge the existence of a divine being or beings since these do not exist in the first place. Causes and effects keep the wheel of samsara turning – not any deity. Non-religious people might respond by questioning how these kammic consequences are decided in the absence of any controlling entity. They might also question the fact that one being's actions might have negative consequences for another. Is this fair?

- Some non-monotheistic religions take the view that God/the gods have positive and negative qualities – and that this duality keeps the universe going. Some regard the universe as being filled with positive and negative forces which mean that good and bad things happen. This is in balance – and some argue that divine beings maintain this balance.

A non-religious person might argue that still this does not seem to account for the randomness and apparently uneven spread of good and evil in the world. For example, at some times, and in some places, there seems to be a lot more evil than good around. Why should any generation or group of beings experience more suffering and evil than any other? Why is the balance of good and evil not constant throughout time and according to where you live? And if divine beings have good and bad qualities, then are they really worthy of our interest and attention?

So, the key argument is that God can and presumably would want to stop suffering and evil but apparently does not. Some would argue that no matter how you look at it, God cannot be 'let off the hook' for the existence of suffering and evil. They exist, so either he cannot or does not choose to do anything about it, or he doesn't exist.

However, others would argue that there are two perfectly reasonable responses to the claim that God is responsible for suffering and evil. The first is that God is not responsible – humans are. God allows humans to make free choices and this brings suffering and evil into the world. This will be considered in the next chapter. The second response is that natural suffering and evil are part of the natural consequences of natural laws which God can't change on a whim. Natural laws require that certain causes lead to certain consequences – God cannot intervene in this, or nothing in the natural world would make sense.

Personal Reflection

* *Do you think that the existence of evil challenges belief in a God (or gods)?*
* *Do you think that the three qualities usually attributed to God are helpful?*
* *Could God/the gods have good and evil qualities?*

Apply your learning

Active Learning

1. In groups of four, have a debate about the problem of suffering and evil. One of you should be devil's advocate, where you probe and challenge the other three. These three should each represent one of Omnipotence, Omniscience and Perfect Goodness.
2. In Judaeo-Christian traditions, the apparent nature of God seems to vary from loving and kind to vengeful and violent. In addition, in Christianity, some argue that the God presented by Jesus is very different from the God presented by the Old Testament. In groups, carry out some research into examples from Judaeo-Christian scriptures of the different natures of God presented. Can you reach any conclusion about the agreed nature of God within Judaeo-Christian traditions?
3. In some religions, deities are presented as, on occasion, having good and bad aspects (or personifications). Carry out some research into this and create an illustrated display of your findings.
4. Create an A–Z of suffering and evil which explains religious views and responses. For example, 'A is for Angry, which God seems to be when he smites the Egyptians with a run of misfortunes …'

Investigate

Find out more about:

➤ different religions' descriptions of the nature of God/gods
➤ personifications of evil across different belief systems
➤ practical ways in which religious and non-religious people respond to suffering and evil
➤ the wheel of samsara and beliefs about kamma (karma)
➤ religious beliefs about the intervention of God/gods in the form of miracles – and responses to these views.

For each of these, report your findings in a manner of your choice. This could be a written report or presentation – in the form of tables, graphs and charts – or as the source of material for a class debate or discussion. You should select a method for your report which is most appropriate for the aspect you are investigating.

Check Your Understanding

1 What benefits and drawbacks might there be if God removed all suffering and evil?
2 Explain what is meant by omnipotence.
3 In what ways is the problem of evil a possible challenge to the idea that God is omnipotent?
4 How might a monotheist respond to the challenge that the existence of suffering and evil presents to omnipotence?
5 Explain what is meant by omniscience.
6 Is the problem of evil a challenge for God's omniscience?
7 What possible criticisms are there to the idea of omniscience?
8 What might a monotheist mean by saying that God is perfectly good, and why might the problem of evil be a challenge to this?
9 What might be meant by saying that suffering and evil are illusions – and what's your view on this?
10 Is God/the gods worthy of our attention if they have good and bad aspects?
11 In what ways does the apparent randomness of suffering and evil challenge religions – and how might religions respond?

Analyse and Evaluate

1 'The problem of evil does not challenge belief in God, it simply challenges some of the qualities religious people give to God.' Discuss this claim.
2 Analyse the view that the problem of evil is a greater challenge for monotheistic faiths than for non-monotheistic ones.
3 'The greatest challenge to belief in God/gods is the apparent randomness of suffering and evil.' Discuss.
4 How successfully do religious views respond to the existence of suffering and evil?

Are humans responsible?

9

No, I wouldn't say it was my fault – she made me do it. All slinky and all that, she cuddles up to me and says, 'This is a really delicious piece of fruit. Want some? I've had a taste – it's nice.'

'Where did you get it?' I asked, and she answered … all innocent-like,

'That tree over there.'

There was something about that tree that made me a little jumpy, and then I remembered:

'Oh for goodness sake, you know we're not meant to eat stuff from that tree.'

'I know,' she said, 'but it just looked so enticing, glinting in the sunshine like that, and besides, there was this serpent.'

'A what?' I replied. 'What serpent? Where? I've never seen a serpent.'

'Well, I have,' says she. 'The serpent said, in a smooth and velvety voice, "Go on, just take one piece of fruit from the tree. I can assure you it is exceedingly tasty."'

'But we were told to avoid that tree.'

'What harm can it do? One little piece of fruit. The tree is groaning with delicious fruit. You'd be doing it a favour, taking a bit of the weight off its branches – and besides, who would notice?'

'But he might, and then he might not be happy.'

'But he gave you the choice. Why should he get to be annoyed because you didn't choose what he wanted? Is he going to control you like that forever?'

'I suppose you're right.'

She plucked one little fruit from a low branch – it would soon have fallen off anyway. So she took it and offered it to me, and I, OK I admit it: I gave in. I took it, and it was nice. Look, it's a piece of fruit, it's not exactly the end of the world, is it? I mean, he might be a wee bit upset, but it's not like everything's going to change from now on because of one wee bit of fruit …

Human responsibility: the key argument

Essentially, the argument is quite simple: humans make choices and sometimes these choices lead to suffering and evil. God is not responsible for our choices. If we choose to do something which leads to suffering and evil for ourselves and/ or others, we cannot pin the blame on anyone but us. God could stop us from doing certain things but that would take away our freedom – which is a key feature of being human and, some would argue, of God's relationship with humans. Remember that this free will argument possibly only really applies to what we refer to as 'human evil', not 'natural evil' (such as an earthquake), as explored in Chapter 8. Again, however, it's not that simple because some things we would call 'natural evil' might have been caused completely or partly by human actions. For example, a raging storm resulting in death and destruction might be considered to be natural evil but if climate change caused by human activity (as some would argue) is part of the cause of that storm, then natural evil could also be considered to be human evil.

The Judaeo-Christian story of the Fall

In the book of Genesis, the creation of the universe is quickly followed by the story of the breakdown in the relationship between humanity and the creator God. In this story, God creates man and woman and puts them in a paradise where every need is met and where there is no evil, pain, suffering or, indeed, anything negative. These humans have complete freedom to do what they want except for one thing: eat from a particular tree. Sadly, eat from this tree is exactly what they do and as a result they are banished from paradise and punished for their actions. In particular, the man is punished by now having to work for a living and the woman is punished by pain in childbirth. This disobedience and banishment signifies that the relationship between the creator and the created has broken down and that this disobedience has consequences.

The meaning of the story

Some religious people consider this story to be literally true: there was a Garden of Eden, two first humans (Adam and Eve), a real tree and a talking snake with a bad attitude. Others consider the story to be metaphorically or symbolically true – with each element of the story representing some broader concept or idea. For example, the first two humans represent all humanity, the tree and fruit represent awareness of themselves and their power to choose to go their own way rather than God's way, and the snake represents either an evil force from outside or their own internal desires and wishes.

No matter whether a literal or symbolic interpretation is accepted, the meaning behind the story is generally agreed to be as follows:

- God makes a perfect universe and a perfect Earth.
- He puts humanity on this perfect Earth and their life is perfect.
- Humans are given freedom to behave as they will, with one requested restriction – that they avoid action which leads to them rejecting God.
- Humans do not obey this restriction and choose to go their own way rather than God's way.
- The relationship between God and humans breaks down and human life becomes a struggle.

Religious people will also add to this understanding three other important concepts:

- The disobedience of the first humans brings sin, suffering and evil into the world – so, in a sense, suffering and evil are our responsibility.
- This sin, suffering and evil affects all creation, not just humans.

⟩ Throughout human history, God continually tries to re-establish the relationship he had with humanity at the start by calling on humanity to engage in the right relationship with God (the one which existed at the start).

Therefore, according to this story – however it is understood – human disobedience is the cause of suffering and evil in the world, and humans remain free to choose how they live their lives on a daily basis. This freedom can have good or bad consequences for the individual and for others.

Talk Point

According to this story, were the first humans really free?

Some challenges to the story

Regardless of whether this story is taken to be literally or symbolically true, there are some criticisms of the story. These can come from within religions, as religious people struggle to understand the meaning of the story, or from non-religious people, for whom the story is filled with contradictions and lack of reasonable argument.

Some of the issues are as follows:

⟩ Why did God give freedom but place a restriction on it? As you may have experienced, telling someone not to do something often increases their desire to do it! (For example, try not to think of an onion. No, go on, don't think about an onion. Think about anything else except an onion …) Why did God put what were perhaps unrealistic limitations on freedom?

⟩ Why give freedom and then punish a free choice? You're either free or not – and if you are going to be punished for your free choice then perhaps you were never free in the first place.

⟩ What's with the serpent? It's bad enough that you're trying to restrain yourself and be obedient, but then you are presented with something that teases and tempts you to do wrong.

⟩ What about forgiveness? Maybe God should have understood the humans' free choice – especially as they were influenced by a smooth-talking snake. Maybe he should have let them off with a warning. Was his punishment a little overly harsh?

⟩ Why should the disobedience of the first humans affect everyone and everything thereafter? It seems a bit unfair that birds and tortoises should suffer because of human disobedience, and perhaps equally unfair that you and I should suffer for the choices of these first humans so long ago.

⟩ Isn't God partly (or completely) to blame for the disobedience of humans? If God is all-knowing, then he must have known what choice humans would make – so perhaps the whole 'giving a choice' thing is ultimately a bit of a pantomime. Even if he genuinely did not see the disobedience coming – and that would be a problem for believers in God – he still created humans with the potential for disobedience – so is his design at fault?

⟩ God is present in the story and humanity is fully aware of his existence, and yet still chooses to disobey. In today's world, very few religious people claim to see God, and some even claim never to have had any experience of God – it's just what they believe in. So obeying what you think God wants when you don't see and/or experience him is a little different from disobeying when you can actually chat with him.

Of course, religious people would say that the free choice had to be exactly that – completely free. If there was not the possibility of at least two choices then it would not have been free at all and would be meaningless. The free choice brought its own consequences which logically followed the choice. The punishment was a logical consequence of the action and, though assigned to God, the fault for the punishment lay not with God but with humanity's wrong choice.

Religious people will also add that God continues to try to turn the first disobedience on its head and re-establish the relationship. This happens through God's direct intervention – such as in the Exodus story, or through his representatives on the Earth in the form of prophets and chosen people throughout the ages. Christians argue that God even sent his own son to suffer on our behalf so that we could re-establish our relationship with him by following Jesus and accepting his actions to turn around the disobedience of the first humans.

Talk Point

If God sent Jesus to suffer and take away sin and suffering, why is there still suffering in the world?

Why is free will so important?

For religious people, the story of the Fall highlights the central importance of free will in human action. Free will is crucial because without it, humanity would be required to enter into a relationship with God and to think and behave in certain ways. This would mean it would be hard to think of humanity as anything special at all – it would just be God's puppet. For religious people, this freedom is what makes us what we are. However, and here's the trouble, freedom of choice must be linked to the consequences of the choice. If it was not, then it would not be real freedom. For example, if I throw an egg at you, it has to follow the course of my throw – and if my throw is accurate, it will have to hit you. Sorry. If the egg was miraculously knocked off course every time, then in what way is my freedom to act really free? Religious people argue that humans were the peak point of creation, and one of the unique features of humans is their ability to make free choices.

Now, the really tricky bit is this: every free choice has a range of potential consequences. These might be very negative consequences for a range of people and/or other things but they have to happen, otherwise the choice was not really free in the first place. This means that suffering and evil can and do occur as a result of our free choice.

In terms of natural evil, we are free to choose where and how we live. If we choose to live on the rim of a volcano and it erupts, killing us in the process, we can hardly complain about it. It would be a funny old world if we decided to live somewhere and a voice boomed out of the heavens … 'No, not there … because …' That would be a very unpredictable world indeed.

As for human evil and the suffering it causes, we have to be able to put our choices into action or else they are not free choices – that's just the way it is. It's an unavoidable consequence of our free will.

Talk Point

Is freedom more important than removing suffering and evil?

Challenges to the free will argument

▸ **Why is free will so important?** Why is it more important than taking away suffering and evil? This is perhaps especially true where one person's free choice has a negative impact on another person. Why couldn't God give us free will to do anything which affects only us, but limit our free will when what we do might have consequences for others? And, when something bad happens, is it enough to say that it's because of free will and there's nothing really to be done about it?

▸ **Why does God intervene sometimes and not at other times?** In what way does it harm our freedom if we never knew that he had intervened? Perhaps God could let me throw that egg at you without interference, but perhaps he should intervene if someone is about to inflict serious harm on someone else. Who would know? Of course, many religious people believe there are occasions where God does exactly this – in the form of miracles. (There's a lot of discussion on this in the next topic.) Why he chooses to intervene sometimes and not at other times is something only he knows and has to be accepted as a matter of faith. Non-religious people might question why we have to accept all these things on faith. Why couldn't God let us think we have free will even if we didn't? This would be a little naughty, but might it not be preferable to all the suffering and evil which exists in the world?

▸ **Why doesn't free will apply to everything?** For example, none of us is free to choose not to die. This will happen to us all in one way or another but why, if free will is so important, are we not free to choose *not* to die (or to become invisible or to fly, etc.)? And why are we not free to demand that God makes his physical presence known to us? Perhaps freedom isn't all it's cracked up to be.

▸ **Why do we continue to be punished for the free choice of the first humans (or for subsequent rejections of God by other generations)?** This is perhaps the central challenge to the free will argument. Why, when a person accepts God, re-establishes the relationship and turns the disobedience of the first and subsequent humans on its head, is that person not excused from all suffering and evil?

▸ **Why does a good God continue to allow Satan/Shaytan to exist and do his unpleasant work?** Some religious people retain a belief in the existence of this evil force or person, which acts to direct us towards evil. Surely it's tough enough for humans to make good decisions without Satan being allowed to stir things?

Determinism

Determinism is the idea that everything that will happen inevitably happens. There are different views about determinism and different kinds of determinism.

▸ **Pre-determinism** This is the view that some external agent – generally God – has already mapped out the future. Therefore we are not free, since the future has been set and is unchangeable. Anything we do which looks like an act of free will is just an illusion, since we could not have acted in any other way because the future is set already.

▸ **Multiple determinism** Some take the view that a range of options for the future are possible, so we remain free to choose which of these we want. Some philosophers argue that this is not really determinism.

▶ **Psychological determinism** Some take the view that while we appear free (and make what appear to be free choices), if you traced every possible contribution to our 'free choice' you would find that we could not have chosen anything other than we did – and therefore are not really free. For example, your genes, upbringing and life circumstances all contribute towards you making one choice rather than another. So you appear to make a free choice when, in actual fact, your choice has been determined by all the many things which have come before your decision, and you cannot avoid the influence this has on you.

▶ **Soft and hard determinism** Some follow the idea of 'soft' determinism where behaviours and choices are determined because the many things which precede them are most likely to lead to one choice rather than another – although we are still free to choose one thing rather than another. Others accept a 'hard' form of determinism where we have no free will (or only an illusion of one) since everything is decided for us by factors we do not control.

The very practical issue with determinism is that, if it is true, it takes away all our responsibility for any choice and with it all responsibility for any consequences of our choice. If true, it would mean that Adam and Eve, however we understood them, were not, in fact, responsible for their choices and therefore God's response to them eating the forbidden fruit was incorrect. If so, this would bring into doubt religious ideas about the Fall and its consequences. It would also have serious implications for kamma, since if we are not really free to choose then we cannot be held responsible for our actions. Therefore it's a little unfair that kamma – good or bad – follows our actions, as they weren't free actions in the first place. However, this brings in the further complication through the idea that humans have moral agency and therefore can indeed have an impact on kamma.

Non-religious people would reject any suggestion of determinism by God, since they reject the idea of God. Many religious people would also reject determinism by God since they might consider it the opposite of free will, which is a gift from God. On the other hand, many non-religious people might accept a form of determinism – the kind where a whole range of circumstances conspire towards you making one choice rather than another.

> **Talk Point**
>
> *Do you consider your choices to be free choices?*

The Irenaean theodicy

Irenaeus (*c.*130–202 CE) was one of the 'Early Fathers' of the Christian Church who helped early Christians make sense of their developing Christian beliefs. The problem of evil was an issue then as it is now and Irenaeus developed a theodicy (an explanation of how a good/benevolent God can still exist even though there is suffering and evil). Irenaeus basically said:

▶ Humans were not born perfect but have to grow spiritually towards full spiritual maturity.
▶ The universe is therefore a 'vale of soul-making' which enables human souls to develop fully into all they can be.
▶ Soul development and improvement takes place as a response to suffering and evil which helps us to grow spiritually.

Therefore the issue of suffering and evil is less of a problem for Irenaeus and more an opportunity. When humans were created there were similarities between them and God, but there were also spiritual differences which had to be overcome through our moral choices, our actions and our response to suffering and evil.

Talk Point

What do you think of the idea that suffering and evil are ways to test our soul?

Responses to the Irenaean theodicy

In addition to questioning the existence of any soul, Irenaeus' theodicy might be also challenged in the following ways:

▶ Why didn't God make humans perfect in the first place? Why this need for spiritual development?

▶ If humans do develop this spiritual perfection, when does it happen? Can individual humans develop it during their lifetime? If, instead, it applies to all humans, how long must the human species wait for this perfection to be in place?

▶ Will humans (or individual humans) be spiritually equal to God when this perfection of the soul has been achieved? If so, what might this imply?

▶ Why does the test of our souls have to be so horrible? Couldn't God have found another way to test and improve our souls which was less unpleasant? And what about humans who have different life-spans and different opportunities to develop their souls? For example, what chance does a stillborn baby have to develop its soul?

The Augustinian theodicy

Augustine of Hippo (a place, not an animal!) (354–430 CE) also developed a theodicy. He argued the following:

▶ Suffering and evil are the logical result of humanity's free choice which resulted in the Fall.

▶ Suffering and evil caused by the Fall affect all humanity forever and all creation too.

▶ Evil is not a thing, but the absence of a thing. (Augustine referred to it as a 'privation'.)

▶ Evil is the result of the misuse of free will.

Responses to the Augustinian theodicy

In addition to questioning whether the Fall happened (either literally or symbolically), Augustine's theodicy might also be challenged in the following ways:

▶ Why did God give humans free choice if he knew they would abuse it?

▶ Why should all humans forever suffer for the original choice and why should all creation suffer?

▶ Why didn't God create beings who were completely free but also unable to make bad choices? This is a logical impossibility, but if God is omnipotent then he must, by definition, be able to make things happen which are logically impossible.

▶ Suffering and evil may seem like the absence of things but they are very real. Try telling someone who is experiencing great pain and suffering that what they are actually experiencing is the absence of peace and happiness …

For many religious people, suffering and evil are the result of free will and therefore the responsibility of humanity. It is simple cause and effect, and God does not and/or cannot intervene because to do so would remove free will. Removing free will would be an even greater wrong than allowing suffering and evil to continue. Consider this: many religious people believe that there is a heaven. In heaven, there are heavenly beings who are perfectly free. But there is no suffering and evil in heaven. If this is possible in heaven, why not on Earth?

A Buddhist perspective on free will

It is clear that the existence of free will is not a challenge to belief in God for Buddhists because they have no God (or gods). For Buddhists, all beings are free to make choices about moral behaviour or anything else. Therefore, for Buddhists, free will explains, in part, the existence of suffering and evil but it isn't a defence for the existence of God in the same way that it is in monotheistic faiths. Buddhists believe that we constantly re-shape and re-design the skandhas ('patterns') which combine to make an individual. Nothing stays the same and all our choices have kammic consequences which can be far-reaching and very unpredictable. Human evil can be both the result of kammic consequences and the cause of further kammic consequences. For Buddhists, wrong choices and their consequences are what maintain the endless cycle of samsara.

Summary

The key argument we have explored in this chapter is that humans cause suffering and evil, not God. God could choose to limit our choices when they would result in suffering and evil but he does not do this in order to protect our free will. As a result, suffering and evil exist but the responsibility lies with humans, not God. In fact, some might argue, if God removed our free will so we could not choose actions which would lead to suffering and evil, then that lack of freedom could itself be considered suffering and evil – so it's a no-win situation for God. On the other hand, some might argue that God could remove only our ability to make choices which lead to suffering and evil for ourselves and/or others, while still allowing us to make other choices. If he did do this, how would we know he had done it? If we did not know that God had removed our ability to make choices which would lead to suffering and evil, where's the problem?

Personal Reflection

* *Do you think preserving free will is a good reason for suffering and evil?*
* *How important is it for the free will defence for the existence of God that the creation story is literally true?*
* *Should God cancel free will?*

Apply your learning

Active Learning

1 Create an exhibition of the lives and views of Irenaeus and Augustine, illustrating how they responded to the problem of evil.
2 Develop a set of questions about the story of the Fall and then attempt to answer them.
3 Write an imaginative story about the day that free will is taken away from humans.
4 Write a script for an imaginary diary entry where God considers whether or not he should remove free will from his creation.

Investigate

Find out more about:

➤ how the free will argument is presented/dealt with in a religion other than Christianity or Buddhism
➤ different interpretations of the story of the Fall
➤ how the story of the Fall is represented in art/music/drama
➤ the life and times of Irenaeus
➤ the life and times of Augustine of Hippo
➤ samsara and kamma (karma) in religions other than Buddhism.

For each of these, report your findings in a manner of your choice. This could be a written report or presentation – in the form of tables, graphs and charts – or as the source of material for a class debate or discussion. You should select a method for your report which is most appropriate for the aspect you are investigating.

Check Your Understanding

1 Describe what happens in the Judaeo-Christian story of the Fall.
2 What is the difference between a literal and symbolic interpretation of this story?
3 Explain what religious people take to be the meaning of the story of the Fall.
4 What religious and philosophical questions are raised by the story of the Fall?
5 Describe two possible challenges to the story of the Fall.
6 Explain your view of one of the challenges you gave in your answer to the previous question.
7 How do Christians think Jesus is linked to the story of the Fall?
8 What different views exist about the importance of free will?
9 Describe three challenges to the free will argument and explain your view on each of these challenges.
10 What is determinism and how does it link to the problem of evil?
11 How did Irenaeus deal with the problem of evil?
12 What are the similarities and differences between Irenaeus' argument and that of Augustine?
13 What is the role of free will in Buddhism and how is it linked to the problem of evil?

Analyse and Evaluate

1 'The free will defence for the existence of God successfully responds to the problem of evil.' Discuss this claim.
2 Analyse the view that maintaining free will is more important than the removal of suffering and evil.
3 'God cannot remove free will. That would be logically impossible.' How far do you agree with this statement?
4 Assess the view that the challenges to the free will defence for the existence of God should lead to the rejection of the defence.
5 'Since all our choices are determined, the consequences of our actions are not ours.' Discuss how far this claim supports or rejects the challenge of the problem of evil.

Now, I understand that suffering and evil are bad things – don't get me wrong. No one can deny that they are horrible and cause great hardship around the world and always have. You can't reason them away like they don't matter – and you certainly can't do that with someone who is currently experiencing them. So how do I cope? Well, it's all very simple really. Suffering and evil will one day come to an end when we get to heaven. There is no evil and no suffering there, and in that place you will suffer no more. Your faith, your life, your actions, God's grace – whatever qualifies you for heaven I don't know, but I do know that one day I will be there and that all suffering and evil will be forgotten. But all that doesn't mean I don't work to alleviate suffering and evil every day.

I, too, understand the horrors of suffering and evil. Yes, they can seem pointless, and I think sometimes they are. But life is a cycle of birth, death and rebirth – suffering in themselves. Kammic cause and effect: no more, no less. Now, I know that explaining to someone that the evil they face or the suffering they experience is the result of kammic consequences may be correct, but it might not be the right thing to say to that person at that time – skilful means, you see. However, I think we all have the potential to escape all suffering and evil through escaping from the endless round of birth, death and rebirth. Nibbana is open to all of us – some call it moksa, or release. It is possible, and it helps me make sense of the reality of suffering and evil. But all that doesn't mean I don't work to alleviate evil end suffering every day.

No, I think there is nothing after life, nor some great ending. Suffering and evil will come to an end, but that will be because I am no more, not because suffering and evil are no more. Is this a depressing thought? Of course not, since I will be released from suffering and evil. At the end of life there will be nothing and, of course, I am sad that I will come to an end, but after my ending I won't be sad any more, since I won't be any more. Yes, the joys and pleasures of life will have come to an end, but so, too, will the troubles and sorrows. But all that doesn't mean I don't work to alleviate suffering and evil every day.

Talk Point

Might all suffering and evil come to an end after this life is over?

Does the problem of suffering and evil matter?

Some would argue that the problem of evil matters even more than any of the other issues covered in this component of your Higher RMPS course. Creation/evolution, arguments about the first cause and so on are all very interesting, but some might argue that they can be a little remote from our everyday experience. Suffering and evil, on the other hand, are very immediate and definitely *not* remote. They can affect individuals in very direct and difficult ways, and they can and have changed the course of individual lives and of history itself. Suffering and evil are serious matters in a great many ways – and present a real challenge.

A challenge for religious people

- Suffering and evil present a direct challenge to the existence of an omnipotent, omniscient and perfectly good God, since it is difficult to accept the existence of such a being in the face of suffering and evil.
- For non-monotheistic faiths, evil is a challenge because it suggests a duality in the qualities of gods. For atheistic faiths, the challenge lies in the extent to which we are free to escape the cause and effect of suffering and evil.
- Suffering and evil pose real challenges for individuals in trying to make sense of them and why they happen. For religious people, they can often be the most serious challenge to their faith.
- Suffering and evil present a challenge to the nature of human beings, our purpose in and response to life. Are we really free? Why did God make us with the potential to do evil? Is evil part of human nature and, if so, what does that say about God's design?
- Suffering and evil present a challenge to the very fabric of nature. Why do natural systems have to lead to pain and suffering? Is there no other way for the laws of nature to act? What role does God/the gods play in all this?
- How should religious people respond to evil? Fight against it – with the possibility of perpetuating evil? Not resist it – which could mean vulnerable people are not protected, and would mean that evil 'wins'?

A challenge for non-religious people

- The existence of suffering and evil might present a challenge for individuals to make sense of them. Why does the development of life seem to be such a struggle? Was there no other way for life to evolve? And why must nature be so violent? Is it not possible for natural systems to develop without accompanying suffering and evil?
- What are the causes of evil and are they part of human nature? Is life therefore some kind of failed experiment?
- Are humans really free to make choices or is everything determined by causes which are often out of our control? Does such determinism apply equally to other beings?
- How should non-religious people respond to evil? Fight it? Accept it? Investigate it? Control it? Is there a right way to respond to suffering and evil which brings benefit to our species and/or our environment?
- Does the fact that humans cause suffering and evil suggest that putting our 'faith' in humans alone is misguided? Given that some humans seem to behave in awful ways, might it not be unreasonable to hope for the existence of some divine figure who can put it right for us?

10 CAN RESPONSIBILITY FOR SUFFERING AND EVIL LIE WITH BOTH GOD AND HUMANS?

105

Suffering

A challenge for religious people

As religion may mean accepting something despite or without rational grounds for belief (or in addition to this), does the unavoidable existence of suffering present a challenge to religion?

- Some religious people have answered 'yes' to this, and have therefore abandoned their life of faith. It is possible that many people who lose their faith do so not in response to abstract arguments (though this does happen) but in response to immediate and unpleasant events. Becoming seriously ill, losing a loved one, despair at the bad things happening in the world – all can lead to loss of faith. This loss can be temporary or permanent and can lead to an improved life or a more impoverished one according to each individual.

- Many religious people will answer 'no' because their religion does not require them to see suffering as a challenge but instead to consider it either as the natural order of things or as a way to grow and develop. Suffering, in this sense, has positive aspects, or at least neutral ones, so is no cause for losing faith.

- Of course, the vast majority of people will respond that suffering is not a challenge to faith because that is the whole point of faith. You believe no matter what. Yes, bad things happen, but that's the way things are. Living by faith means accepting this without any need for further consideration.

A challenge for non-religious people

Similarly, suffering can present a challenge to someone who lives life without any religious belief.

- Suffering is a challenge, perhaps because it seems so unreasonable. Its randomness and apparent pointlessness make you wonder what it's all about. It might be perfectly all right to come up with clever arguments about the necessity, inevitability or purpose of suffering, but that doesn't help when you are experiencing it.

- Most people who live without religious belief are likely to argue that suffering is far from desirable but it is unavoidable. The reasonable conclusion is that it is an inevitable part of the state of the universe and the beings which inhabit it. That we don't like it and want to avoid its consequences should not be considered a reason to leap into a position based on faith – where you simply accept it as having some greater purpose and therefore make sense of it that way. Suffering probably has little purpose (other than providing an opportunity for people to do good in response, though some non-religious people might agree with religious people by seeing some 'value' in suffering). In fact, perhaps 'purpose' is a term we simply shouldn't use in relation to suffering. Things happen without any purpose all the time – perhaps suffering is just one of them.

Talk Point

Do you think it is possible to benefit from suffering?

Evil

A challenge for religious people

Remember that evil can be the cause of suffering, the result of suffering, a purposeful willed action on the part of a person, or the result of natural forces. So the challenges for faith in relation to suffering also apply to evil, with a few additions.

- Some religious people's faith in God will be challenged by evil because, one way or another, God is perhaps partly (or completely) responsible for evil. If all creation is God's work, then evil in the system must also be God's work – and therefore his responsibility. This applies whether you think evil has a purpose or not, or whether you think it is the result of human free will or not. At the end of the day, God made it all and so he is accountable for the system.

▶ If evil is the result of natural forces, this still presents problems because these forces are part of a system of laws and principles designed by the creator – so responsibility for them must lie with him.

▶ If evil is the result of an evil being or personification of evil, it has to be asked why God permits this.

▶ For some people, the biggest challenge is perhaps the lack of real clarity about what evil might be 'for'. Many religious people take the view that the universe and all life in it is ordered and structured by God for a purpose – that God has 'a plan'. The problem is that he has not shared this plan with us and so it is not clear how evil does or might contribute to that plan. It's a bit like taking a test when you don't know what the course has been about.

▶ A big challenge for some is the sheer practical challenge of holding on to faith in the face of great evil. During the Holocaust, for example, it would have been very difficult to hold on to faith in the face of the horrors witnessed. Some held on to it and others did not. Similarly, when faced with great evil, it can be difficult to hold on to the possibly abstract concept of faith.

▶ For those religions without belief in a God, it might still be difficult to square up the existence of evil with their faith. For example, it would be easy to wonder why kammic consequences have not 'caught up' with those who do evil things. Why don't they seem to get what they deserve?

A challenge for non-religious people

The existence of evil can also be a challenge for those who base their lives on rational thinking and reasonable responses.

▶ Evil seems to be unduly random – why is it so? If everything in the universe is as random as this, you might wonder why you should live any kind of good life since there doesn't seem to be any link between being a good person, living a healthy lifestyle, acting nobly towards others and avoiding random evil.

▶ Evil really does make you wonder if the universe is somehow flawed – and if humans (and all living things) are as well. Some people might argue that the apparent lack of order and structure in the universe – and the fact that it is filled with evil – leads to the conclusion that you can live your life in any way that you like. What is the point of studying, reflecting, analysing and taking a reasoned approach to life if, at the end of it all, evil will randomly visit you and inflict things on you quite unrelated to how you have lived your life so far? What incentive is there for anyone to do any better?

▶ Could the existence of evil in the universe simply lead to the view that the most effective way to deal with it is to be more evil than the next person? Most religions argue that you should fight hate with love, but reason might lead you to the conclusion that it is more effective to fight hate with stronger and more effective hate (unpleasant as that sounds).

Talk Point

What do you consider to be the biggest challenge presented by the problem of evil?

Responsibility for suffering and evil: God, humans or both?

There are various possible responses to this question:

1 God *or* humans are responsible alone.
2 Neither God *nor* humans are responsible.
3 A combination of the first two points.

But before we look at the answers we first have to consider the question of 'responsibility'.

10 CAN RESPONSIBILITY FOR SUFFERING AND EVIL LIE WITH BOTH GOD AND HUMANS?

107

Is anyone or anything 'responsible'?

The word 'responsible' implies cause and effect – someone or something does something and this leads to suffering and evil. However, many of the causes of suffering and evil are simply natural processes. Illness, disease and natural disasters happen according to the laws of physics. Does it make sense to say that anyone is 'responsible' for these? Is this any different from saying that someone or something is 'responsible' for the rising and setting of the sun?

Of course, natural suffering and evil might be made worse by human actions. For example, diseases can spread more rapidly where there is poor sanitation, and this may be more likely to affect those who are poor and vulnerable. Although no one could be considered 'responsible' for the existence of a disease-causing virus or bacteria, perhaps doing nothing to prevent the conditions which enable it to spread more rapidly means someone or something is responsible – and this could equally well land at the door of God or humans. So before we proceed, we really need to think about what 'responsible' might mean in this case.

God

God is not responsible

- Buddhists, for example, take the view that there is no such thing as God, as do Humanists and atheists. If this is the case, then the idea of God being responsible makes no sense. No God – no responsibility.
- Those who do believe in God, no matter what shape or form this God takes, may still feel he is not responsible for human-caused suffering and evil. This could be linked to the free will argument: God allows humans to make free choices but can't be considered responsible for those choices. So the responsibility for suffering and evil lies not with God but with human choices, the natural consequences of which must be 'allowed' to proceed.
- In relation to natural evil, God cannot be considered responsible because the natural laws of physics must be allowed to work as they do naturally. God cannot change the laws of physics every time they threaten to result in suffering and evil, otherwise we would live in a universe which made no sense. Therefore, regrettably, God must allow natural suffering and evil to exist – since they are sometimes the unavoidable outcome of natural forces – but he is not responsible.
- In some religions, God's responsibility is thought to be lessened by the existence of 'opposite' forces such as Shaytan/Satan/the Devil. These religions would take the view that these 'opposite' beings are responsible for suffering and evil, not God.

God is responsible

For those who believe in the existence of God, suffering and evil could be considered a real challenge to his existence and/or his nature, leading to the inescapable conclusion that he is responsible.

- By definition, God is the most powerful being there is, therefore he has the power to allow or not allow anything. To suggest that Shaytan/Satan/the Devil is responsible rather than God raises two important questions. The first is why God would have created such a being in the first place. Religious views tend to argue that God did not 'make' the Devil, but that the Devil was a good being who rejected God. The second question is why, even if this is the case, God allows this rebellious being to continue to exist and, what's more, to continue to behave in unacceptable ways by causing suffering and evil. Surely God could either bring an end to this evil being or at least control it more effectively. In many ways it looks like God doesn't control this being when he could and therefore God could be considered to be responsible for its actions and the consequences of its actions.
- In relation to human-caused suffering and evil, God could still be considered to be responsible. Again, God is the most powerful being there is – he could prohibit all human actions which lead to suffering and evil but apparently does not. Some would argue that the free will argument is not good enough. Why is free will more important than bringing an end to suffering and evil? And could God not allow us to have the illusion of free will, while not permitting anything which might lead to suffering and evil? Those who argue that God is responsible might well say that he could and should 'shut down' our ability to make choices which lead to suffering and evil without us ever

knowing that he had done it. However, we make these kinds of decisions all the time therefore either he can't stop us (in which case he is not an all-powerful God) or won't stop us (in which case he's not a perfectly good God). If you want to believe in a God who is all-powerful and perfectly good, you're perhaps going to have some trouble accepting all these contradictions at the same time.

Humans

Humans are not responsible

▷ Given what has been said above, humans could easily pass the responsibility for suffering and evil on to God. Only a being such as that can bring an end to suffering and evil – doing so is far beyond human capability, especially in relation to suffering and evil brought about by natural causes. Humans can and do make progress in fighting disease and illness but, given that he could end these things in an instant, they are God's responsibility and not the responsibility of humans. Humans also can't make much of an impact on natural causes of suffering and evil, such as earthquakes and tsunamis, but God could, so again they are his responsibility.

▷ Of course, some would argue that humans are very much responsible for suffering and evil caused by humans because they make the choices in the first place. But others would argue that by not intervening to sort this out (by not allowing humans to make such bad choices), God becomes responsible for the consequences of those choices.

▷ Some might argue that humans are not responsible because the concept of 'responsibility' is not a meaningful one. This is especially true in relation to natural causes of suffering and evil because they 'cause' themselves. However, even in relation to human-caused suffering and evil, perhaps all the many complex factors which lead to a human decision mean that simple human responsibility is hard to pin down. For example, some would argue that human actions are the result of many complex factors, many of which are beyond our control (some might argue that this brings into question how far any one of us is 'in control' of ourself!), so to simply conclude that each of us is responsible ignores the many contributions from outside influences leading to our decisions. In effect, our environment, upbringing, personal circumstances and so on are responsible, not us.

Humans are responsible

▷ For those who do not believe in a God, there is no one else to blame for suffering and evil but us.

▷ For those who believe in God, some would argue that 'passing the buck' to him is just silly. We can't wait for a divine being to do something about suffering and evil – we have to do it for ourselves. Each person has to take responsibility for their own actions and not wait for a God to do it for them.

▷ It is true that humans have limited control over natural forces and the suffering and evil they can cause but having limited control doesn't mean we have no control. Some argue, for example, that human actions can affect the natural world and have consequences which bring about suffering and evil. There are many possible examples of this but one is the contentious issue of climate change. Many take the view that human actions are causing climate change which in turn is resulting in more storms, floods and other negative environmental consequences. If these lead to suffering and evil for humans and the natural world, and they are a result of our actions, then we can be considered responsible for them.

▷ Many would agree that the factors which lead to any human action which causes suffering and evil are very complex. However, some would still take the view that although they are complex, the final decision about our behaviour lies with us. We can't blame our circumstances, our upbringing or anything else – we have to shoulder the responsibility. Human actions which lead to suffering and evil are our responsibility as individuals and as a species.

Can the responsibility for suffering and evil lie with both God and humans?

For those who believe in the existence of God, the simple answer to this is 'yes' for the following reasons:

▷ The causes of some types of suffering and evil might not be in human control and anything not in human control is, by definition, in God's control, therefore he is responsible for 'this kind' of suffering and evil.

10 CAN RESPONSIBILITY FOR SUFFERING AND EVIL LIE WITH BOTH GOD AND HUMANS?

109

▶ Humans are responsible for suffering and evil caused by humans. Although God could intervene, the free will argument means that he does not. Therefore, God is not responsible for our actions; we are.

▶ Although God is not directly responsible for our actions and their consequences, he is the one who provides the free will in the first place (and who created us with the potential to exercise our free will in potentially harmful ways). Therefore, since he allows our free will and made us what we are, he must share the responsibility for our actions or, as some might argue, take full responsibility for them.

Let's go right back to the start of this argument and imagine God or humans have the power to remove all suffering and evil from our world and choose to do so. Would that ever be logically possible, or would it involve such a change to the laws of physics that nothing would ever make sense again?

Talk Point

In what ways do/might religious and non-religious people work to reduce suffering?

Personal Reflection

✳ *Do you agree that suffering and evil are the biggest challenges to religious belief?*
✳ *What compatibility can religious and non-religious people reach about suffering and evil?*
✳ *What do you think of the view that suffering and evil will one day be no more?*

Apply your learning

Active Learning

1. Based on what you have learned in this topic about the similarities and differences between religious and non-religious perspectives, write your own rhyming poem about these similarities and differences, referring to the challenge of suffering and evil for each perspective.

2. Write your own script of a dialogue between two religious people. One of them believes that we can make sense of suffering and evil now, while the other thinks we will only have 'answers' in the afterlife.

3. Create a series of flash cards with images which represent the issues you have studied in this topic. Then use the cards as stimuli for group discussion.

4. Create your own word cloud using the text in this topic. (Do not cheat by going online!) What are the key words raised by this topic and in what proportion? What does this tell you about the key issues raised by the problem of suffering and evil?

Investigate

Find out more about:

- ➤ views of the afterlife in monotheistic religions
- ➤ views of the afterlife in non-monotheistic religions
- ➤ Humanist views of the afterlife
- ➤ views of the afterlife from other cultures and traditions/belief systems
- ➤ different views about the 'value' of suffering.

For each of these, report your findings in a manner of your choice. This could be a written report or presentation – in the form of tables, graphs and charts – or as the source of material for a class debate or discussion. You should select a method for your report which is most appropriate for the aspect you are investigating.

Check Your Understanding

1 How might suffering challenge religious belief?
2 In what ways might the existence of evil challenge non-religious beliefs?
3 Why might some think that the problem of evil matters and others not?
4 Why might someone argue that God is responsible for evil?
5 Could religious and non-religious people agree that suffering has 'value'?
6 What are the differences between the ways that monotheistic and non-monotheistic faiths might approach the problem of evil?
7 In what ways might religious and non-religious people agree about responses to suffering and evil?
8 How might a religious person explain the belief that God has 'a plan' and how might suffering and evil fit into this?
9 Can you accept the reality of suffering and evil and still hold on to a faith?
10 How can different beliefs about life after death (or no life after death) possibly affect views about suffering and evil?
11 In your view, does it make any sense to say that anything is 'responsible' for suffering and evil?
12 In your view, is God responsible for suffering and evil or are humans responsible (or both)?

Analyse and Evaluate

1 'Only God can bring an end to suffering and evil. He does not. Therefore he is responsible for suffering and evil.' Discuss this claim.
2 Analyse the view that humans are entirely responsible for the existence of suffering and evil.
3 To what extent are suffering and evil a challenge for non-religious people?
4 'The free will argument means that God is not responsible for suffering and evil.' Discuss.

ARE MIRACLES
REAL?

Religious explanations and evidence

11

The Galilean Sea Scrolls were unexpectedly discovered in a stall in Barrowland, Glasgow, in mid-2016. After some reluctance, and only after they had promised to buy some super-soft bath towels ('two pairs for a pound'), 'Big Mick' sold them to a group of very excited professors from Glasgow University. The professors took the scrolls to the University and began the laborious process of translating them from Aramaic. The scrolls turned out to tell very ordinary stories of very ordinary people who lived around the Sea of Galilee almost two thousand years ago. The scrolls give a tantalising glimpse into life then, and have created shockwaves around the world as they seem to make reference to key figures and events of the time. The extract below records a conversation between Rebbe and Dan, two rugged and ordinary fishermen working in the Sea of Galilee. As they tidy up their nets, they chew over the latest fishing – which hasn't been good …

(NB [...] indicates words or phrases which were missing or obscured in the scrolls and so could not be translated.)

Dan: [...] fishing today wouldn't thou agree?

Rebbe: Verily. I cast my nets yonder and hauled naught but a sprat, an octopus leg devoid of the octopus and a sandal.

Dan: Thou shouldst make use of that sandal since thy own sandals are an embarrassment.

Rebbe: *Thou hast spoken in truth, Dan, but thy apparel is far from the latest fashion.*

Dan: Mine apparel doeth the job, Rebbe, unlike thy nets today – for surely they were holy.

Rebbe: *I have indeed sanctified these nets with thanksgiving.*

Dan: No, Rebbe, I mean thy nets are filled with holes.

Rebbe: *It is ever thus, for if there were no holes then the sea wouldst not pour through them, leaving the fish entrapped behind.*

Dan: In truth, Rebbe, but thy holes are much greater than any creature which mightest call this sea their abode. Perhaps thou shouldst mend thy nets oftentimes, instead of [...] around in the sun on [...]

Rebbe: *It is good for the soul, Dan, to rest mine [...]*

Dan: But poor for thy welfare, Rebbe, for thou art making few enough shekels as it is, and greater sweat from thy brow would surely increase thy yield.

Rebbe: *Truly it is a warm day today, and my brow doth sweat indeed, verily I am pure dead boiling.*

Dan: By 'sweat of thy brow' I mean thy toil, Rebbe – thou must strive more to fill thy nets, for they shall not fill themselves.

Rebbe: *But Dan, they doeth. It happened to [...] Perhaps we, too, should offer up a burnt offering.*

Dan: Obliged, Rebbe, but I have sworn never to eat thy cooking again since previously [...] and I [...] so greatly that [...]

Rebbe: *No, Dan – we should maketh an offering for good fish in return, just as fisherfolk on the other side of the lake have done. It is said they hauled their nets which overflowed with plump fish – so great their boats nearly sank.*

Dan: Thy boat is often in danger of floundering when thou art in it, Rebbe. Perhaps thou shouldst [...]

Rebbe: *No, Dan, it is said that their haul itself was a miracle.*

Dan: Rebbe, when thou catchest any fish I often think upon it as a miracle.

Rebbe: *No, a miracle which cameth about [...]*

Dan: Now calmeth thyself, Rebbe. Thou art being unreasonable – why would anyone ask a miracle just to gather sardines?

Rebbe: *To showeth the power [...]*

Dan: I fear thou hast been draining amphorae whilst celebrating Dionysus over-much of late, Rebbe.

Rebbe: *Thou knowest that not to be so, Dan, for the last time I [...] and I was then told [...]*

Dan: So these fisherfolk did haul a divine catch thou sayest?

Rebbe: *So sayeth some, Dan – though the truth be hidden from our eyes and perhaps it is naught but fishy tales – though tales I believe, Dan, tales I believe.*

Dan: But, Rebbe, thou wilt believe anything, like when [...] for thy wits are surely slow.

Rebbe: *Why hast thou so little faith, Dan? Why doubtest thee so greatly?*

Dan: Surely I have faith, Rebbe – I have worked with thee all these years [...] Miracles?! Soon thou wilt be telling me that there is one who strolleth across that Sea in his sandals [...]

Talk Point

Do you believe in miracles?

What is a miracle?

Whether it happened long ago or yesterday, whether it is recorded in scriptures or on YouTube, a miracle may have a variety of definitions. Perhaps the one most likely to be suggested by religious people is that a miracle is an interruption to the normal laws of physics, and that the cause of this interruption is divine action by a God or gods. Miracles might be direct or they might be through the actions of *intermediaries* – others through whom God acts (or gods act). For religious people, miracles might be easily identified, or they might have to be *inferred* – which means that we have to read into some action a miraculous cause. So, for example, imagine you were crossing the road and a bright, shining, winged angel appeared before you and blocked your path just as a speeding car would have killed you. A religious person would obviously identify this as a miracle, and it would be hard to avoid that conclusion. But imagine that just as you go to step out on to the road, you think you hear someone calling your name so you stop – and this means you don't walk into the path of the car. You might think of that as a miracle too.

It is important to remember that the word 'miracle' is often used to describe things which are not claimed to have any element of divine intervention, such as amazing recoveries from illness, lucky escapes in accidents and so on.

Religious people often say that a miracle is a response to an appeal to God (or their gods) – perhaps through prayer. However, they would also accept that miracles can happen 'out of the blue' – for some reason known only to God (or the gods). Experiencing an incident that you consider to be a miracle is likely to have a significant impact on your belief, and on your life. Religious and non-religious people have claimed to have experienced miracles (although they will usually account for them differently). Within most religions there are claims of miracles in many of the sacred texts/scriptures, which tell of the power of their God (gods), or of powerful spiritual forces. There are, however, many different views within religions about miracles – about their existence, why they might take place and how we should respond to them.

Miraculous fishing

The Bible describes a miracle catch of fish (John 21:1–25). At the crack of dawn, Jesus – after his resurrection – asks his disciples if they'd had any luck fishing. (It was quite dark and the disciples didn't know who he was at first.) When they told him they hadn't, he told them to cast their nets on the right side and, miraculously, they hauled in more fish than they could handle – 153 to be precise. In fact, this was the second time Jesus had helped fishermen with a miraculous catch of fish. (Another occasion is described in Luke 5:1–11.) These stories include three claimed miracles: a miraculous amount of fish; a miraculously intact net, even though it was full of fish; and a miraculous post-resurrection appearance by Jesus in one of the stories.

For some Christians, the main point of the miracle described in John 21 is that it shows that Jesus' power remained, even after his resurrection from the dead. (And, of course, it showed that he had been resurrected in the first place.) It also showed that he still cared for his disciples and wanted to feed them – both physically and spiritually. Christians also believe that this is one of Jesus' 'nature miracles' – showing that he is fully God because only God would have power over nature in this way. Christians believe that this story is another way in which the Bible teaches them about the nature of Jesus/God and also about the kind of relationship he wants to have with people.

Miracles in Judaeo-Christian scriptures: New Testament

There are a number of different types of miracle in the Bible. In the New Testament, they are almost always carried out by Jesus or, in the case of Pentecost, by the Holy Spirit. There are also occasions where it is claimed they have been carried out by Jesus' disciples and the Apostles.

Miracles over nature

These might be calming storms, catching fish, walking on water or even turning water into wine – or, less positively, causing a fig tree to wither on the spot. These miracles exist to show the power of God (through Jesus and the Holy Spirit) because only a divine being could control nature. These are direct events carried out by figures in the New Testament, but they could raise questions about why these particular acts and why these situations. One possible difficulty here is that those who witnessed these events might have no need of faith – because the miracle proved the power of God (although you'd have to believe your own eyes, of course). For some, this is a problem, since faith has the potential to be 'cancelled out' by definite proof.

Miraculous healings

Jesus healed people of a wide range of illnesses – including epilepsy, blindness, leprosy, deafness and paralysis. He even restored the severed ear of a high priest's servant. Not only that, but on three occasions Jesus is claimed to have raised people from the dead – including Lazarus, who had been dead for four days. It is claimed that Jesus did not even need to be physically present to carry out healings. For Christians, these miracles show, once again, the power of God over natural forces of illness and disease, but they also show God's compassion for those afflicted by them. However, they do raise some issues. For example, why heal the specific people in each story – why not everyone afflicted in that way? Why raise one person from the dead and not another – especially as all three of the people raised would have had to die again at some point? Some might consider it a little odd to put someone through the experience of being raised from the dead – only to die again later – just to make a point.

Miraculous provision of food

Jesus fed five thousand people using a small number of loaves and fish. Christians believe that this shows God's power over nature, but also that he cares for the everyday needs of people by providing them with food. Again, however, it raises difficult issues. Why the people in this particular situation and why not anyone else who may have been hungry – or, indeed, starving – at that time?

Miraculous powers over evil spirits

On a number of occasions, Jesus casts out demons from people who are being controlled by them, showing his compassion for those afflicted in this way and that he has power over evil in the form of evil demons. This raises a number of issues about the existence of evil demons and why God might allow these beings to inhabit people in the first place. It also raises difficult questions which continue to be discussed in Christianity – how far certain things might be caused by evil spirits and what to do about this. In the past (and sometimes today), it was firmly believed that certain physical and mental illnesses were the result of demonic possession and that the 'treatment' for these illnesses was to remove the demon.

Miracles in Judaeo-Christian scriptures: Old Testament

A range of miracles are claimed to have happened throughout history. These miracles cover a range of positive events, such as power over nature, miraculous provisions of food, protection from harm, and even a talking donkey (Numbers 22:21–35). However, there is also a darker side to the miracles described here, because many involve miraculous defeats of the enemies of the Israelites – or terrible punishments carried out on them, such as the ten plagues of Egypt (Exodus 7:20, etc.). There are also killings for disobedience (for example 2 Samuel 6:6–7), and some very curious miracles, such as the Sun going backwards (2 Kings 20:9–11) and 42 boys killed by bears brought about by a prophet's curse (after the boys had made unkind comments about his bald head) (2 Kings 2:23–24). Many of these miracles are also claimed to show the power of God, though it is likely that religious people will find it difficult to explain the specific purpose of some of them.

Talk Point

Do you think that Christians and Jews are required to believe in the miracles in the scriptures?

Miracles in other religious scriptures

Buddhism

In Buddhism, it is sometimes claimed that the Buddha could multiply himself, fly (sometimes to other worlds) and read minds. It is even claimed that on one occasion he transformed the top half of his body into fire and the lower half into water. In addition to this, it is claimed that he calmed a very angry elephant. It is said that the elephant knelt down in front of him whereas before it had been rampaging dangerously. However, it is also said that the Buddha was wary of miracles and instructed those of his followers who had miraculous powers not to exercise them in public. Miracles in Buddhism do not come from a God or gods (as these do not exist according to the Buddhist point of view), but from the

mind. It is claimed that some Buddhist leaders throughout history, and even today, have performed miraculous acts due to the power and focus of their minds. In these cases, the purpose of the miracle is not to prove divine power over anything (since Buddhists do not believe in a divine being), but to show that the mind can cause amazing – miraculous – things to happen when it reaches a suitable state through meditation and other Buddhist practices.

Hinduism

There are many instances of miraculous events throughout the history of the Hindu religion. Often these miracles happened in relation to divine beings, such as the god Ganesh, whose head was removed but miraculously replaced with that of an elephant; and a story where Lord Siva saved the Earth from flooding by holding the river Ganges in a knot in his hair. As well as miracles linked to divine beings, Hinduism is filled with miracles said to have been carried out by holy people who have acted as channels for the power of Hindu deities. Sometimes these miraculous acts are the result of psychic powers claimed to have been brought on, for example, by focused yogic practices. There have been claims of miraculous healings and visions, as well as miracles where statues weep milk and other manifestations of divine power.

As in all religions, there are devotees in Hinduism and Buddhism who accept all of these miracles as factual accounts, but there are others who interpret them in a wide variety of other ways – more of that in the next chapter.

Issues raised by scriptural miracles

1 There are some issues about scriptures in general. Some religious people believe that their scriptures came direct from God/their gods and so contain stories and teachings which are completely true. Others take the view that scriptures are the product of the writers, the time and places in which they lived, and their cultural outlook on life. Scriptures are handed down through the generations, sometimes by word of mouth and sometimes by copying written text. In both cases, it's possible that changes and errors creep in so that as time moves further away from the original story or event, the less reliable our present-day version of it might be. Add to all of this the possibility that scriptures were written for a purpose and so may contain stories and events designed to communicate that purpose. For example, the writers of the New Testament were convinced that Jesus was the Son of God/God on Earth, therefore they wanted to prove this by reporting the miracles he performed (which only a God could do). So we must be aware that this was the intention of the writers and of the possibility that the writers themselves may have been re-telling stories they had heard, rather than recounting things they had personally witnessed.

2 The purpose of many of the scriptural miracles might raise questions. Clearly, some were designed to show the power of divine beings over nature, but others seem a little more odd and lacking in any clear purpose. Some seem strange – such as raising some people from the dead (but not others) only for them to have to go through death all over again. Turning water into wine might also be considered an odd way to show power. Also, some New Testament miracles depend upon the belief in demonic possession as a cause of physical and mental disorders – an idea that most people nowadays would reject.

3 There is cruelty in some scriptural miracles which might raise questions about the deity who is responsible for them. For example, in the Jewish scriptures, God kills all the firstborn children in Egyptian households, sparing the children of Israelites. It is easy to see how some might question the nature of God which such an act suggests. In the New Testament, Jesus curses a tree which withers immediately. What could be the message of this miracle?

4 Many miracles seem to have happened in the past and no longer happen today. There were spectacular miracles, such as the closing of the sea over the Egyptians pursuing the Israelites, Jesus walking on water, miraculous escapes from certain death and so on. These seem to be less prevalent nowadays (and some would argue no longer present at all), which leads people to ask why they happened in scriptures but do not happen today. There have been many situations in modern times where people and whole communities have been in great danger and have prayed for a miracle – with little apparent response.

Talk Point

Should religious people treat scriptural miracles as true or as products of time and place?

Religious explanations for scriptural miracles: strengths and weaknesses

Strengths

▶ For religious people, the scriptures are usually thought of as 'divinely inspired'. This means that they come from God/ the gods and so contain the truth. There are, of course, many different understandings of how far they are literally or metaphorically true within and across religions. Many religious people take their scriptures at face value, so when they describe a miracle, that's what happened – exactly as described.

▶ Miracles in scriptures show the power of God/the gods/religious figures. They are there to show that the agent who causes the miracle is a divine being or has been given the power to do so by a divine being (or that natural activities have been orchestrated by the divine being or his agent). Remember that religion is based on faith, and so accepting the truth of a miracle is an act of faith. If you start to doubt the truth of miracle stories in the scriptures, then what next might you start to doubt? Of course, some religious people argue that miracle stories in the scriptures do not describe actual changes to the laws of physics, but are to be understood metaphorically – as part of a message rather than an actual event. So, for example, some might argue that the miracle of the loaves and fish was not a miracle where food was created out of nothing, but a miracle because when people saw food being shared they decided to share their own food too – this was the miracle.

▶ For religious people, the key strength of scriptural miracles is that such stories support their beliefs about and claims for their God/gods/important figures. There is no need to 'prove' them since they should be accepted in faith – based on a belief in an all-powerful divine being(s).

Weaknesses

▶ The major weakness with religious explanations for miracles in scriptures is that they cannot now be proved (or disproved). They are sometimes pretty extraordinary claims (raising a man from the dead, parting the seas, etc.) so they would need some equally strong evidence to support them. However, since it is claimed they happened long ago, it is difficult to find any evidence to support or reject them. Some religious people do try to do so, such as looking for evidence of a great flood and remains of Noah's ark, but conclusive proof remains difficult to achieve. In the absence of solid evidence, what are we to make of claims of miracles?

▶ Another weakness is, of course, the fact that religious arguments often rest on accepting miracles in scriptures as acts of faith. Some miracles seem perfectly reasonable, such as healing people who are sick, but others seem a bit less reasonable, such as striking down enemies. Should we accept both of these as a matter of faith? Many religious people do, since that's what religion means for them. Others find it more difficult to accept some things on faith and/or some things compared to others. Many religious people believe that while faith is important so, too, is applying your thinking skills in relation to religious claims. Miracles go against the laws of nature – we should generally expect the laws of nature to apply in all situations and so it would be unreasonable to accept that scriptures tell of amendments to the laws of nature. Why then? Why not now? Why that miracle? Why for that person? Some religious people might argue that scriptural miracles raise more questions than they answer and so, perhaps, it makes more sense not to focus on them too much.

Modern-day miracles

Many religious people are keen to point out that miracles are not just restricted to the stories in their holy books. Many claim that miracles occur today, and that these miracles still show the power of God (gods) or show the power of faith and belief. Belief in miracles is not limited to any particular group within any religion – all religions have followers who believe in the literal truth of miracles today. However, it is probably true to say that within some religions, there are groups who are more widely accepting of miraculous events than other branches of the faith.

Miraculous experiences and events

There is widespread belief in miracles within Christianity, though it is probably most commonplace within Evangelical, Pentecostal and Charismatic Christian groups. One well-known example is the 'Toronto Blessing'. This began in a church near Toronto International Airport in Canada and saw people fall down, laugh and/or roll about uncontrollably, make animal noises, stagger around as if they were drunk, dance and so on – signs of the 'gifts of the Holy Spirit'. Often this began with the laying on of hands and people falling backwards as if struck. Some Christian groups refer to this as being 'slain in the Spirit' and it occurs across a number of Evangelical/Pentecostal/Charismatic Christian groups. Many Christians accept these behaviours as miracles – evidence of being filled with the Holy Spirit – and they can be accompanied by visions, healings and a range of gifts of the Spirit, such as speaking in tongues. Many other Christians are a little more cautious about such experiences, and whether they are truly miracles from God or not, while some are very sceptical indeed. However, as a Christian, it would be odd to accept that miracles in the Bible were real but that miracles today are not – though there is some variation in thinking about this within the faith. In many other religions, too, there are miracles which result in a range of 'miraculous' behaviours and activities – from feats of great endurance (walking on hot coals) to other examples of 'spiritual power', such as mind reading, out-of-body projection, and so on.

Healing miracles

As well as these dramatic 'gifts of the Spirit', Christianity today is filled with belief in many different types of miracle. Within Roman Catholicism, for example, miracles are often claimed to be the result of prayer. This can lead to people from the past being declared a saint because a prayer to them has resulted in a miracle – proof of their sainthood. Most branches of Christianity accept the possibility of miraculous healing from illness and disease. Sometimes these take centre stage in acts of worship while at other times they happen quietly and without any accompanying demonstration of faith. These miracles continue the belief that God/gods can and does intervene to bring an end to pain and suffering. Other religions also accept the possibility of miraculous healing – and these can be carried out with or without the involvement of a special 'healer'.

Miracles of deliverance

Some religions propose that there are miracles of deliverance, such as being spared from a terrible disaster or accident – perhaps the only person to survive a plane crash. Sometimes these miracles are accompanied by other spiritual features – someone might claim that 'an angel' pushed them out of the way of an oncoming car, or appeared just before they made a 'miraculous' recovery from illness. Some will also argue that being delivered from their 'old' life to a 'new' life is a form of miracle – resulting, for example, in turning away from crime or drugs, and so on.

Visions and miraculous happenings

In Catholicism, there are miraculous visions of Mary and other key figures in the faith. Other branches of Christianity have also reported miraculous sightings of religious figures, angels or other divine beings. Sometimes these visions are linked to particular events – the flag of Scotland (the Saltire) is said to have originated as a miraculous formation in the sky prior to a successful battle. Most religions have reports of some kind of miraculous vision or happening which might include sightings of deities or other divine beings.

As well as sightings of divine beings and other beings, there are reports from all religions of weeping and bleeding statues, physical manifestations of faith such as the stigmata, moving statues and the face of religious figures appearing in ordinary objects – such as the face of Jesus on a slice of toast, or the sacred name of God in Hinduism, Om, appearing inside an aubergine.

Issues raised by modern-day miracles

1   Some argue that the dramatic nature of many modern miracles calls into question whether they are divine acts or the power of suggestion, frenzy, expectation, and so on. In situations where miracles are commonplace in worship, such worship is usually very animated and physical and brings about high levels of emotion. Some argue that this might bring about a state of mind which leads people to experience or think they are witnessing divine power. Many experiences, such as the 'Toronto Blessing', appear very strange in their results and some Christians therefore question their origin and purpose. Others are equally sceptical – even within Christianity – of some of the 'fruits of the Spirit', such as speaking in tongues. This is a feature of some Christian groups but is absent in most branches of Christianity. In other religions, there might also be scepticism about how far specific feats of endurance are really gifts from divine beings or something else entirely.

2   Some argue that healing miracles raise a number of important questions. For example, instead of being grateful for a healing miracle, perhaps we should ask why the person became ill in the first place. And why is it claimed that some people benefit from healing miracles while others do not? Are some more worthy than others? Do some not have 'enough faith'? Does God/the gods choose some to benefit and not others – and, if so, why? Would it be better if God/the gods ensured that people didn't become ill in the first place, and therefore didn't need a healing miracle?

3   Some healing miracles seem to be carried out by those specially 'chosen' for this task. Why those people and not others?

4   Why do some people benefit from miracles of deliverance and not others? There have been occasions when earthquake victims have been found alive under piles of rubble, many days after the earthquake, when rescuers had almost given up hope. These are sometimes cited as great miracles, but the number of people who are found dead usually far outnumbers those who survive. Is this an 'anti-miracle'? There seems to be a randomness about the whole process, with some people 'miraculously' avoiding harm, while others don't. Why are some chosen to be spared while so many others are not?

5   We need to consider why people have visions or miraculous religious experiences and think about what else might be happening. Why would a God/gods favour one group over another in battle and send a miraculous sign? Why do some people have visions of religious figures and others do not? What is the ultimate purpose of any miraculous vision?

6   Why would God/the gods choose to communicate with humans in such bizarre ways as weeping statues and faces of religious figures appearing in everyday objects? Many such weeping statues have been shown to be the result of chemical reactions as well as trickery and other illusions. If some can be explained away, why not all?

It is probably fair to say that while religious people generally accept the possibility of miracles, in practice many are sceptical that they actually take place – for a variety of reasons. We will explore different interpretations of miracles in more detail in the next chapter.

Religious explanations for modern-day miracles: strengths and weaknesses

Strengths

▶   Just as with miracles in scriptures, some religious people will argue that miracles today still come from God/the gods and so are true. Similarly, there are many different understandings of how far they are literally or metaphorically true within and across religions. Many religious people accept such events as seen and experienced – so when they describe a modern-day miracle, that's what has happened.

- Similarly, too, modern-day miracles show the power of God/the gods/religious figures. They are there to show that the agent who caused the miracle is a divine being or has been given the power to do so by a divine being (or that natural activities have been orchestrated by the divine being or his agent). Religion is based on faith, and so accepting the truth of a miracle is an act of faith. If you start to doubt the truth of miracles, then what next might you start to doubt? Of course, some religious people argue that modern-day miracles do not describe actual changes to the laws of physics but are to be understood metaphorically – as part of a message rather than an actual event.
- For religious people, the key strength of modern-day miracles is that such events support their beliefs about and claims for their God/gods/important figures. There is no need to 'prove' them since they should be accepted in faith – based on a belief in an all-powerful divine being(s). It is also important to accept them because it shows that God/the gods/religious figures did not 'call a halt' to miracles once the scriptures had been written, but continue to do deliver them today.

Weaknesses

- The major weakness with religious explanations for modern-day miracles is that they are very difficult to verify or falsify. When something is claimed to be miraculous, there is unlikely to be a full team of scientists on hand to record, measure and test what has happened. This means that claims of modern-day miracles are still subject to the memory recall of those who saw or experienced them, and memory recall can be notoriously poor. Some miracle claims have been tested scientifically after the event. In some cases the tests provided alternative explanations for the miraculous event, while others have been less conclusive. This generally relates to miracles which have involved a physical change involved, such as a 'miraculous healing' or something like a weeping statue. It is very difficult to apply any kind of test where a miracle has been in the form of visions and voices. Some might argue that scientific tests are not possible because some miracles are 'spiritual experiences' which cannot be tested for conclusive evidence. So, as with scriptural miracles, conclusive proof remains difficult to achieve. In the absence of solid evidence, what are we to make of claims of modern-day miracles?
- Another weakness of the religious explanations for modern-day miracles is that they could always be playing 'catch-up' with scientific progress. Many things which might have been considered miracles in the past can now be explained scientifically. Might modern-day miracles also be explained scientifically in years to come?
- Another possible weakness which could apply to modern-day and scriptural miracles is the apparent randomness of it all. For example, it is not unusual to hear that someone who has survived a terrible accident calls their survival 'a miracle'. This might overlook the fact that others involved in the accident may not have experienced a miracle. Why would some be selected for a miraculous intervention and not others? Similarly, many claims to have been cured of illness by a miracle raise the important questions of why a person became ill in the first place (could this be an 'anti-miracle'?) and why only some seem to get this 'miraculous' treatment and not everyone. The discussion here is not a straightforward one, but it does raise the question of why miracles are claimed to occur in some situations and contexts, but are troublingly absent in others. Some religious people claim to have had their lives 'turned around' by a miracle, such as turning from a life of crime to living a more considerate life. Although the outcome here is a positive one, it raises questions of why it took something 'miraculous' to turn around the person's life, why their life wasn't heading in the right direction in the first place and how we explain a person turning around their life in the absence of any miraculous event.

Miracles in non-religious settings

Miraculous events and experiences are often claimed to have happened to non-religious people as well as religious people. Some regard these as evidence of a 'spiritual dimension' to life (not a religious one, though the distinction isn't always clear), while others think that they are simply unexplainable. Sometimes such events prompt people to ask deep questions about belief and can lead to them becoming religious or adopting a more spiritual approach to life, or just changing their thinking or way of life. At other times, such occurrences are simply seen as events that we do not yet understand, but for which there will be a reasonable, scientific explanation at some point in the future. For example, some people claim to have had miraculous healings of diseases where no scientific explanation seems to be possible. Some say that these show the limits of human understanding, while others simply claim that the absence of a reasonable explanation doesn't mean that one doesn't exist. Some say that our understanding of miracles is very closely linked to our current understanding of the world. Imagine that you could transport someone from 500 years ago to the present day – what kind of things might he or she think of as miracles? (Mobile phones, TVs, antibiotics, aircraft …)

Issues raised by non-religious miracles

Many of the issues here also apply to miracles in religious contexts.

1   If such miraculous events are beyond rational explanation, does this point to the existence of a spiritual dimension to life? Does this mean that non-religious people might have to reassess their views about the way things are? Perhaps miracles do point to the existence of divine beings. Does this mean that non-religious people need to think again?

2   Is it possible that miracles point to a set of physical laws which have not yet been discovered? This might have nothing to do with any deity but might indicate the existence of things which are not yet part of our understanding of how the universe works. This raises further questions about how far such experiences might be investigated and provide evidence one way or another. Are the tools of science able to investigate miracles? If so, should they? And if not, could they be developed in order to do so in the future?

3   Are such miracles simply mind over matter?

4   Given the fact that religion is not involved, does the context in which the miracle happened tell us anything about how the miracle might be rationally explained? For example, are there rational explanations for the miracle linked to expectation, environment and other factors? Could there be a personality type which is more susceptible to experiencing miracles and/or explaining things as miracles?

Personal Reflection

* *Do you believe in miracles?*
* *If miracles are described in religious scriptures, should we still expect miracles to happen today?*
* *What (if anything) do you think miracles prove? The existence of God/gods? Supernatural powers? Unexplained forces of nature? That the laws of physics are not as straightforward as we think?*

Apply your learning

Active Learning

1 In groups, choose one of the miracles referred to in this chapter. Produce a plan to investigate this miracle. What questions would you ask of whom? What evidence would you gather, etc.?
2 Carry out some further research into miracles in a religion of your choice. Categorise these miracles into groups ('healing miracles', etc.). You can do this for scriptural accounts or modern-day accounts of miracles. Choose an appropriate format to present your findings.
3 How are those who claim to have experienced miracles/visions, etc. generally treated? Produce a piece of imaginative writing where someone in your class claims to have experienced something miraculous. Describe what happens next.
4 Using news reports, images and artwork, create a visual display entitled: 'It's a miracle'. Invite people who view your display to add their comments to it using sticky notes.

Investigate

Find out more about:

➤ different understandings of scriptural miracles in a religion of your choice
➤ scientific explanations for things which are claimed to be miraculous
➤ modern-day stories about those who claim to have experienced something miraculous
➤ examples of people whose lives have been changed by miraculous experiences
➤ the kind of things someone would consider to be a miracle if they were magically transported from the sixteenth to the twenty-first century.

For each of these, report your findings in a manner of your choice. This could be a written report or presentation — in the form of tables, graphs and charts — or as the source of material for a class debate or discussion. You should select a method for your report which is most appropriate for the aspect you are investigating.

Check Your Understanding

1 Give a definition of 'miracle' and explain your view of this definition.
2 Describe two miracles from scriptures which Christians and/or Jewish people would accept.
3 Describe one miracle from a religion other than Judaism or Christianity.
4 For two types of miracle described in this chapter, suggest one possible question that each might raise.
5 According to religious people, what are the main purposes of miracles?
6 What issues might be linked specifically to miracles in scriptures?
7 Describe two types of modern-day religious miracle.
8 Explain one issue which might arise from a modern-day religious miracle.
9 What 'miracles' might be experienced by non-religious people?
10 Choose one kind of 'miracle' and describe how non-religious people would generally explain it.
11 What possible impact does/might a miracle have on religious people?
12 What could be the impact of a miracle/'miracle' on someone who is not religious?
13 What are the strengths and weaknesses of religious explanations for modern-day miracles?
14 What are the weaknesses of religious explanations for scriptural miracles?

Analyse and Evaluate

1 'Miracles in religious scriptures must be treated with caution because they are a product of their time and place.' Discuss this claim.
2 Analyse the view that miracles cannot be accepted as spiritual events in a scientific age.
3 'Miracles provide more questions than they do answers, and so should be ignored by religious people.' Discuss.
4 To what extent do miracles raise the same issues for religious and non-religious people?

Non-religious explanations and evidence

I am now going to do something really rather strange in this book. Something I've never done before in any of my books. I am going to read your mind ... No, really, I am. I want you to get a picture in your mind of all your living relatives – they must be living, for only they will create an energy pattern in your mind that is strong enough ... I am going to reach into your mind and describe one of these relatives to you. Are you ready? Here we go. Prepare to be amazed, and a little spooked. I'm good at this and always have been ...

OK, I'm getting a picture now. It's a little fuzzy, so concentrate a bit more on all your living family members ... That's better, the picture is clearing now – though not for some of you. I think you are letting your minds wander too much ... Yes, here it comes.

I'm seeing a man, he's older than you. His name begins with a 'J'. I think it is maybe James, or it could be John. I think he might be an uncle.

Let's stick with Uncle John perhaps, but it could be James, names are sometimes the hardest part to read from a distance. He is quite a big man, and he works ... I see him outdoors ... There is height involved in his work – could it be scaffolding? Building trade of some kind? There are other men in his line of work – they laugh a lot ...

He's a bit grimy and dusty – perhaps that is because of his job, or maybe he's just a bit untidy. He's got a fair bit of stubble – he doesn't shave often enough – or is it just a dirty face? He carries a little too much weight – he should be fitter for the job he does.

I sense that he has, or has had in the past, some trouble with his back, at least he complains about it on occasion. He has maybe had an injury, or perhaps a strain, and it means that sometimes he doesn't move as quickly as he could. It could be his leg, actually.

I think your uncle used to smoke – he may have given up, or perhaps he now has one of those odd e-cigarette things. He's always being told to give up but he just laughs this off ...

He likes to think he's a funny man, too, and is forever cracking jokes. At least, he thinks he is funny and he thinks they are jokes ... Sometimes his jokes are more likely to make you groan than laugh.

Well ... now that picture is fading ... But I'm getting a picture of another relative. 'Margaret' or 'Mary' I think she's called – there's an 'M' in her name somewhere ...

Talk Point

Have you just experienced a miraculous case of mind-reading?

Miracles – making sense of experience

A miracle is an alteration to the known laws of physics – an interruption to the way things normally are. A lot of religious people claim to have experienced a miracle. Many religious people believe in them but many do not. Several scriptures across many religions tell of miraculous events. Many religious people accept these completely, others accept them partly and others do not accept them at all. Non-religious people may agree that people think they are experiencing a miracle when they are actually experiencing something else entirely. So whether people experience miracles or not is a matter of debate, and relates closely to what is claimed about miracles. In the chapter after this one we will explore religious claims about miracles, but first we will consider explanations which see no need for a God/gods/divine being or any special powers or abilities.

Now, it is entirely possible that I wasn't able to read the mind of anyone in your class, but do this in your average class of 30 or so students, and you will usually find at least one or two who are struck by the uncanny similarity to their Uncle John, or James. I should stress that I am not a mind reader of any kind and make no claims to any such power (despite what it says in the text). What you have been reading is a made-up story about someone, which probably gets a 'hit' or two from some people in your class, making them wonder if something amazing is going on. All that the text does is as follows.

- It makes a claim to my 'psychic abilities' which you have no reason to accept, but, equally, no reason to doubt.
- It makes vague, general statements which could apply to many people. How many people in Scotland are likely to have a relative named John or James? What if this story had been read in Japan – do you think as many people there are likely to have a relative named John or James?
- It provides a 'get-out' so as to include more people in the trickery: 'some trouble with his back' could apply to a huge number of people in Scotland, and if not because of an actual medical condition then through complaining about back pain – which could be on a daily basis or a one-off incident.
- It links ideas together to reinforce them further – 'height' links to scaffolding, which might link to building, which can often be a job where it's hard not to get a bit dusty!
- It provides an 'explanation' for failure – explaining that certain aspects of this 'mind-reading' are difficult and that perhaps your own concentration is at fault.

Throughout all of this, the crucial thing is that you have probably tried to impose meaning on the text, and as soon as some of the text seems meaningful, you start to make further links where maybe there aren't any. Why does this happen?

- It's probably true that many people would like psychic mind-reading powers to exist, and so we gladly play along when we are presented with the possibility of them.
- Humans are perhaps 'meaning-seeking' beings. We like things to make sense. We like order and structure, and where it is absent we sometimes impose it for ourselves. For example, when someone hears of a person's death often the first thing they ask is 'What age were they?' They are asking this because they want to build the story of the person – they may follow this by asking what caused their death, how long they had been ill, or where the accident happened and so on. We like to build up a picture of meaning in our world – and with the 'mind reading' above that's exactly what you did – your brain rooted around to find links with the text which are meaningful to you.
- You noticed the things which you thought were 'right' about the text and passed over the things which were not. If you do this in a class, people are amazed by the one or two people who have a relative who matches the description in the text, and completely ignore the other 28 for whom the story is totally irrelevant.

- Humans may have an inbuilt tendency to see patterns where there may not be patterns. Some view this as an evolutionary survival strategy that helps us to sense possible dangers which might be partially obscured in some way. Often we make mistakes about this but, the argument goes, it is better to make some mistakes when there is no threat than fail to notice when there is a threat. So, for example, if we spot a 'face' in an object that turns out not to be a face 99.9% of the time, there's no threat to us and no harm done. But if that face is a danger to us 0.1% of the time then it's a good thing that we spot it. It's worth looking a bit silly the other 99.9% of the time.

Some psychologists have called this 'patternicity' – our tendency to find order and structure, and meaning where there isn't any. They say this helps us cope with life and make sense of it all. It avoids the feeling that everything is random and uncontrolled and that anything can happen – quite scary – and replaces it with the view that somehow it is all ordered and structured, which is more comforting. Children demonstrate this tendency when you read them a story – they get very upset if you change the story (or if it doesn't have a happy or satisfactory ending). Is it possible that adults behave this way too? Is it possible that we impose patterns on things where there is only randomness? The concept of patternicity might be very closely linked to miracles because these are usually, by definition, very strange events. The stranger the event, the more likely we are to impose our own interpretation and pattern on it because otherwise it really challenges our view of the way things are.

What this means is that miracles of different kinds might be interpreted in one way rather than another because of our need to impose pattern and order on the experiences we have or hear about.

Talk Point

Have you ever seen a 'pattern' in something where there was not really any pattern?

Miracles – a matter of interpretation

It is important to remember that religious people usually trust their scriptures, religious leaders and religious experiences. Whether they accept these literally or metaphorically is another matter, but they usually start from the point of view that their scriptures/leaders/experiences are true, helpful and not designed to fool them. So already they are 'primed' to believe what their scriptures say – no matter how strange that might be. They trust their scriptures/leaders/experiences to help them make sense of what sometimes appears to be a senseless world. They trust that their God/the gods have their best interests at heart, are looking after things and ensuring structure and order. This is a comforting thought and therefore encourages further trust in things claimed or experienced. The problem here, of course, is that this might blind them to any inaccuracies and inconsistencies. If religious people accept their scriptures/leaders/experiences as 'having the power', then it is very easy to go from this to always accepting everything that they say, rather than taking a critical approach to them. For non-religious people this presents the same risk as is possible with the 'Uncle John' mind-reading story.

Religious people believe that their God/the gods are very powerful and that they created and control nature – so believing that they can alter nature is equally acceptable. Witnessing a freak of nature which is claimed to be a miracle is quite simple, because all that is required is that you interpret what you see as something which has a meaning and structure imposed from outside – by a divine being or beings. Again, your existing beliefs might lead you to interpret natural events as having a divine influence behind them and so make meaning out of random natural occurrences. This can apply to all manner of miracles – including healing miracles, where spontaneous remission of illness is quickly interpreted as divine intervention, and visions and religious experiences immediately interpreted as divinely orchestrated rather than random happenings.

Talk Point

Why might someone want to believe in miracles?

Non-religious scientific explanations

It's important to remember here that by 'scientific' we mean in the sense of basing our understanding on research, evidence, the interpretation of evidence and so on. Many scientists are also religious people who have a faith – and some religious people who are not scientists will accept scientific findings about a great many things, while still maintaining their religious beliefs. It is important that we don't think of science and religion as some kind of 'Punch and Judy' show where the two are always at each other's throat. Science involves observing, hypothesising, experimenting and verifying. It works on empirical evidence – solid, demonstrable evidence – as well as theories to explain the evidence available. A scientific understanding of miracles would therefore reject accepting them based on faith. Instead, a scientist would produce a hypothesis about a claimed miracle and then gather and test the evidence available – if that is possible. In principle, a miracle (like anything else) must be able to be shown to be true (verifiable) and able to be shown to be false (falsifiable). If it cannot be shown to be true or false, then it is difficult, if not impossible, to approach it scientifically. Bear in mind that many miracles are individual experiences, and it is very difficult to 'get inside' someone's head to analyse their experience!

Miracles claimed in scriptures cannot be directly tested since they happened in the past, though the principles applying to them can still be tested today. Many argue that there are science-based explanations for miracles such as the plagues of Egypt, an example being red algae in the Nile giving the appearance of blood, killing the fish and making the frogs leave the river. Modern miracles can be tested to an extent, depending upon the claim. Of course, it is highly unlikely that anyone experiencing a miracle will call upon a scientist to test it, so we might consider more of a theoretical approach to miracle testing here. In reality, the testing of any miracle claim is unlikely – unless the claim is about a miracle which is *about* to happen. Science offers a considerable range of theories to explain what is actually happening in miracles – if they are not examples of some divine intervention in the laws of nature. Some of these theories are based on physical considerations and others are based on cognitive/psychological considerations.

Possible physical explanations

It is possible that some accounts of miracles are linked to physical disturbances in the body/mind. It is well known that certain conditions can be linked to visual and/or aural (voice-hearing) hallucinations. There is some disagreement within the scientific community as to the causes of such experiences, with some arguing that they are the result of childhood trauma, biochemical factors, or neurological malfunctioning, amongst other possible explanations. Sometimes these conditions can be treated with drugs and/or therapies and the hallucinations cease. This supports the view that they are the result of internal physical processes.

▸ **The causes of such physical disturbances are many and varied.** They include illness/disease; degenerative conditions such as dementia; infections/viruses; trauma and/or accident; stress; genetic/environmental factors; and many other possible physical or psychological origins over which we have no or little control. Such physical conditions can lead to altered states of perception and understanding and so interpreting certain things as miracles – for example, many people in the past (and still some today) who claimed to hear voices might have interpreted these voices as coming from real beings, while others accepted them as a neurological condition. A possible strength of this explanation is that it links 'miracles' to very natural causes, avoiding any need for a 'supernatural' explanation. However, the possibility of explaining some strange experiences in this way does not mean that they all can be.

▶ **Some physical explanations are caused intentionally.** The intention might be to produce an altered state of consciousness. Purposeful activities include taking drugs/alcohol or other substances which have a range of physical and neurological effects; or engaging in activities which lead to an altered state of consciousness, such as repetitive movements, music, or other sensory stimulation or activities. For example, many people claim to have a religious experience when they are in an altered state of consciousness through prayer/meditation or other religious activities. These can be linked to visions and other hallucinations and even to physical manifestations such as stigmata and so on. In some cultures, severe forms of deprivation and sensory stimulation such as self-immolation, sweat lodges and vision quests have led to profound religious experiences and claims of miraculous happenings. Some religions place great emphasis on sensory stimulation of one kind or another as part of their religious practices – and scientists consider the link between this and claims of miraculous happenings to be far more than coincidence. They would question why any 'substances' or 'experiences' have to be in place before someone can experience something miraculous but others would argue that using 'substances' or creating certain contexts does not invalidate any resulting miraculous events.

▶ **Some physical explanations may be the result of causes which are not sought out or manufactured by people.** For example, oxygen deprivation to the brain may result in an altered state of consciousness which leads someone to experience a 'miraculous' event. This can happen as the result of illness/trauma, but can also happen in certain environmental conditions. For example, air pressure is lower at altitude and oxygen levels are lower as a result – there is less oxygen in each breath taken. There have been many documented cases of hallucinations and 'religious experiences' while in places which are high above sea level. Again, this seems like good evidence of a natural explanation for miraculous events but others might argue that it still doesn't rule out some supernatural experience.

▶ **Some scientists have gone as far as to carry out research into how far religious experiences can be manufactured artificially.** The 'God Helmet' is a device which is effectively a crash helmet with powerful magnets. It was developed by scientists to stimulate the temporal lobes in the brain. Some have claimed to have experienced religious and other unusual sensory perceptions when wearing the helmet. Scientists therefore argue that sensing 'divine' experiences happens inside your brain and does not come from any divine being. However, some people might say that even if the God Helmet produces this effect, it does not mean that all experiences of the divine happen inside the brain – in fact, perhaps this is a physical mechanism in our brain which is designed (by God/the gods) for this very purpose.

▶ **Some miraculous events may have a physical cause.** For example, some cases of weeping and bleeding statues have been shown to be caused by chemical reactions and environmental conditions affecting the material from which the statues are made. This leads to liquefaction of the material which may look as if it is tears and/or blood. There have also been cases where the body of a religious person has been 'miraculously' preserved long after their death and, again, in some cases this is thought to be due to natural chemical and environmental processes acting to preserve the corpse. The physical evidence makes this quite a powerful argument in favour of natural explanations for 'miraculous' events but some would point out that there is not a physical explanation in every case.

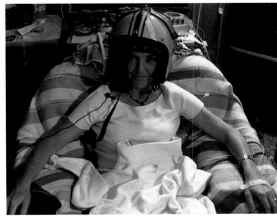

So for some, experiences which link to miracles can have very physical origins. Scientists also consider that miracles can be explained by other psychological and cognitive processes.

Talk Point

Should a religious person reject a miracle if it can be explained scientifically?

Possible psychological explanations

You need to bear in mind that the distinction between physical and psychological/cognitive is not a clear one. Many psychologists take the view that all psychological processes are essentially physical, while others argue that they are a combination of physical, psychological and social processes (leading to the rather snappy term 'biopsychosocial'). There may be a unique combination of physical, psychological and social processes in action in relation to any claimed miracle.

▶ **The power of expectation** For some, this is a major factor in experiencing miracles. Some believe that the power of expectation can make you more suggestible and therefore more likely to experience, or interpret something as, a miracle. In some religious traditions, miracles are expected as part of worship and as part of religious life. Miracles may involve 'gifts of the Spirit' and are proof of your faith and of the truth of your faith. Psychologists argue that expectation and suggestibility are features of many aspects of human behaviour. For example, it is well known that research participants can sometimes influence the outcome of the research without knowing it (or can do so on purpose in order to please the researcher). This is known as 'participant effects' or 'participant bias'. Perhaps this happens to people experiencing miracles – they expect something to happen and somehow cause it to happen without knowing how, or they are so keen to show their faith that they go along with it. This might also be the result of a charismatic leader who (knowingly or not) creates the right 'conditions' for people to experience something that they then think of as a miracle. (See pages 133–134.) This seems to be another strong argument in support of the contributory effects of a range of factors leading to 'miraculous' experiences but, again, some might argue that it does not provide an explanation in every case.

▶ **Placebo effects** Most drug and psychology experiments involve testing the effect of something which the researcher has introduced (an independent/input variable). Those who experience this independent variable are known as the experimental group. There may also be a control group, whose members may experience a different independent/input variable or who may experience no intervention at all. No matter the form of the experiment, the measurable outcome is known as the dependent/output variable. The researcher will then compare the results from

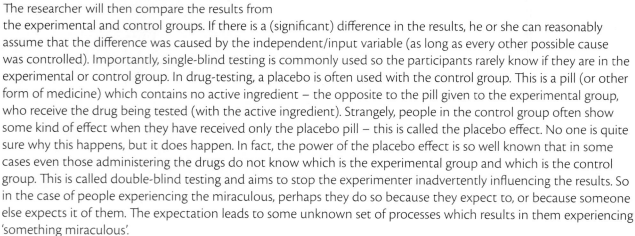

the experimental and control groups. If there is a (significant) difference in the results, he or she can reasonably assume that the difference was caused by the independent/input variable (as long as every other possible cause was controlled). Importantly, single-blind testing is commonly used so the participants rarely know if they are in the experimental or control group. In drug-testing, a placebo is often used with the control group. This is a pill (or other form of medicine) which contains no active ingredient – the opposite to the pill given to the experimental group, who receive the drug being tested (with the active ingredient). Strangely, people in the control group often show some kind of effect when they have received only the placebo pill – this is called the placebo effect. No one is quite sure why this happens, but it does happen. In fact, the power of the placebo effect is so well known that in some cases even those administering the drugs do not know which is the experimental group and which is the control group. This is called double-blind testing and aims to stop the experimenter inadvertently influencing the results. So in the case of people experiencing the miraculous, perhaps they do so because they expect to, or because someone else expects it of them. The expectation leads to some unknown set of processes which results in them experiencing 'something miraculous'.

▶ **Neurological pathways and conditions** All of our experiences, sensations and emotions are, generally speaking, processed by our brain. They are the result of electrochemical processes taking place in our neurons – an incredibly complex collection of brain cell pathways. While we know how neurons work when they are functioning normally, we don't always know what happens when they malfunction. Many psychological conditions and experiences are thought to be the result of disordered (or differently ordered) neurological pathways. This could lead to a range of experiences and sensations, including visions, a sense of well-being or 'religious experiences'. It might also create conditions where the brain manages pain relief or responds to illness/disease in unpredictable ways. So differently ordered neurological functioning might explain what we consider to be miracles. Some might respond by claiming that a miracle can only be experienced through our physical senses so this does not discount miraculous experiences.

- **Inattention blindness** This is a very curious psychological phenomenon, where people quite literally do not see what is right in front of them. One possible explanation for this is that we interpret the world around us in ways which 'blind us' to things which are very obvious. We might focus on the detail and 'miss' the the bigger picture, or we might see the bigger picture, but miss the important details (like that extra 'the' in the middle of this sentence). In other words, sometimes we might see only what we want to, or fail to to see what we don't want to. Could this explain experiencing (or not experiencing) something miraculous (like the second 'to' in the middle of the previous sentence)? Perhaps people seeing 'miracles' are not seeing what is actually in front of them all the time – or, perhaps, they are!

- **Witness reliability** Psychologists are aware that witness testimony can be very insecure. Memory itself is something we 're-construct' each time we retrieve it, and there are a range of factors involved in accurately recalling memory. In some circumstances, psychologists have shown that memories can be 'planted' in people to make them think that something happened when it did not. Perhaps those who experience or witness miracles are not reliable witnesses, and a range of processes take place which lead them to recall and/or report things as miracles. Some would argue that there is no reason why someone would not be able to accurately recall a miraculous experience and, in fact, the unusual nature of them might mean they are more likely to be remembered.

- **Psychological priming** Some psychologists suggest that we can be 'primed' (prepared or made ready) to accept something and/or interpret it in one way rather than another. For example, imagine you are asked to be on the lookout for repeated words in a textbook. Would you you be more likely to spot any repeated words compared the the ones you might have missed in the previous bullet point? Psychologists consider that priming can lead us to think one way rather than another. For example, if you're watching a scary movie and hear a noise somewhere in your house, how much more likely are you to think this noise is something to be worried about, rather than just your house creaking, as a result of the scary movie? Some argue that interpreting things as miracles is linked to whether we are 'primed' to do so or not. This priming might be the result of our upbringing, or the culture we live in, or a set of circumstances created by someone to allow us to experience – or think we're experiencing – something miraculous.

- **Association and reinforcement** Psychologists suggest part of our learning is linked to these two concepts. We learn by linking one thing with another and/or by having an experience reinforced by something else. In the case of miracles, perhaps we associate certain events, practices and so on with miraculous happenings and so are more likely to interpret something as miraculous. The first followers of Jesus thought he was the Messiah, and so perhaps they already associated him with greatness. Perhaps, therefore, they were more likely to interpret what he did as miraculous. Reinforcement is where we are 'rewarded' for our behaviours and so learn to do them again. It could be that in certain circumstances we are 'rewarded' for our actions (and our faith?) with increasingly miraculous experiences. They had been brought up with sacred stories which detailed miraculous events carried out by God or on God's behalf – so they were already 'primed' to believe.

- **Emotional and social factors** Many experiences of 'miraculous' events happen when people are not in their usual state of mind. There can be many reasons for this, but perhaps the key thing is that the people who experience miracles are in a heightened state of awareness and so more ready to consider something to be miraculous rather than ordinary. Add to this the effect of other people around them appearing to experience something. For example, if someone standing beside you claims to see a vision of something divine you might easily dismiss their claim if you can't see anything, but if one hundred people around you claim to see a vision of something divine you might be inclined to go along with their claim even if you can't see anything. Peer pressure, expectation, reinforcement, an altered state of mind – all of these might combine to make you think you are experiencing something out of the ordinary. Some might say that people need to be in such a state of mind for them to be receptive to the miraculous.

- **Charismatic leaders** Some might argue that the influence and actions of strong leaders can help create the circumstances where people experience 'miraculous' things. In some religions, strong and charismatic leaders might encourage 'followers' to go along with an apparently miraculous experience. This is a very complex situation, and there are many reasons why a person might follow a leader, but, again, it suggests that there is a possibility that many factors are involved in experiencing something as miraculous. Someone who believes that God works 'through' certain people (more than others perhaps) might consider that it perfectly acceptable for a leader to 'facilitate' a miraculous event.

- **Tricksters and charlatans and the deluded** It's debatable if this can be considered as a psychological factor, but it is worth thinking about anyway. Perhaps some people who report or claim to cause miracles are simply tricksters. Perhaps they think that fame, fortune, a place in history, or some other reward will follow if they claim to have experienced (or caused) something miraculous. Perhaps followers of key figures in religions made up or exaggerated what their leaders did so as to make them seem more holy/special. It's possible that some people are not tricking others on purpose – perhaps they genuinely believe their experiences, and their conviction about them makes others believe them too. At the start of this chapter, you encountered a phenomenon known as 'cold reading', a process often used by people who claim to have psychic powers. Some such people are tricksters, and perhaps others genuinely believe that they have these abilities. Of course, the existence of charlatans and tricksters does not mean that every experience of the miraculous can be 'explained away' in this way.

Whether the cause of experiencing miracles is physical, psychological or some very complex mixture of contributing factors, for science, miracles are not evidence of the existence of a divine being/beings or any supernatural powers. They have perfectly reasonable explanations which can (or, at some point, will) be demonstrated using scientific methods of enquiry. Therefore, whatever their nature they are explained by science not in supernatural ways, but in very natural ways.

> **Talk Point**
>
> *Do these physical explanations for miracles convince you that miracles are false?*

David Hume

While science aims to investigate miracles using methods of practical research and analysis, philosophers have often responded to miracles based on rational thinking alone. One such response came from the Scottish philosopher David Hume (1711–1776). Hume started with a definition of a miracle as something which is a 'violation of the laws of nature' – in other words, unnatural events which go against the accepted laws of physics. He argued that in our regular experience, the laws of physics seem to work without any alteration and so they are regular, predictable and so on. Therefore it would seem very unreasonable to think that these laws can be altered randomly in some circumstances. Hume argued that it is reasonable to accept that which is most probable. Miracles are, by definition, quite improbable, and therefore it is not reasonable to accept them. When someone claims something to be miraculous, it is safer to assume they are wrong because their claim goes against the majority of our experience, rather than think that the laws of physics have been temporarily suspended to allow a miracle to take place. Hume is therefore weighing up two probabilities:

- The probability that a miracle has occurred.
- The probability that a claim of a miracle is inaccurate.

Hume argued that it is always more reasonable to assume that the report of a miracle is wrong rather than that a miracle happened – so miracles should be rejected.

Hume also argued that witness testimony becomes less reliable as time goes on and so claims of miracles in scripture become weaker the further we are from the time of the claim. He was very blunt when he said that the evidence for (the Christian) religion was 'less than the truth of our senses'.

In addition to this he argued the following:

▶ The reliability of those claiming miracles can be further questioned because there have never been enough claimants who, according to him, were of 'unquestioned good sense, education, learning, reputation and undoubted integrity'.

▶ Humans naturally seek explanations for things which support their need for 'wonder' in the world. Essentially, he claimed that humans have a tendency to attribute to things explanations which are unnecessary other than to fulfil the person's need for a more exciting life.

▶ Claims of miracles are reduced as a society becomes more 'advanced'. Hume argued that miracle claims are more likely to come from 'ignorant and uncivilised people'. As a society becomes more advanced, more reasonable explanations become the norm.

▶ Hume also doubted the individual testimony of those who claimed miracles because, in his view, there will always be those who offer a more reasonable explanation. He also noted that different religions or traditions may have contradictory miracle claims.

Talk Point

How effective are Hume's arguments?

Responses to Hume

Many religious people dismiss Hume's rejection of miracles based on their belief alone. Hume is entitled to his opinion, but that is all it is – his opinion. Many religious people base their acceptance of miracles on faith – believing without the need for evidence. They feel that their religion is true for a great many reasons, and this supports the possibility that miracles are also true (although not all religious people accept them as literally true). In addition to a response based on faith, religious people might add the following:

▶ Our ordinary experience tells us that the laws of physics work in the same ways always and everywhere, but why should we automatically reject something just because it is a 'minority' experience? Is it reasonable to reject something just because it is unusual? Isn't this simply a choice based on your belief?

▶ Even if something is 'less reasonable' than something else (a miracle claim against the laws of physics), there is no automatic reason to assume that the less reasonable thing is less true.

▶ It might be safer to assume that the claim of a miracle is wrong, than that the miracle happened, but it does not automatically follow that the miracle did not happen.

▶ Eyewitness testimony may sometimes be unreliable, but that's not to say it is automatically wrong.

▶ Just because something happened long ago does not necessarily mean that the report of it has become corrupted or misunderstood. Perhaps it happened exactly as described.

▶ What if 'our senses' tell us that religion is true and/or that miracles happen? Should we simply reject them?

▶ Hume takes quite a snobbish line about people's level of intelligence. Should we only accept claims of miracles from people who are very intelligent?

- Perhaps humans do look for more exciting explanations for things but, again, that fact does not automatically make the claims false.
- Hume suggests that societies become more advanced with time. Perhaps this is true and perhaps not. Perhaps less 'advanced' societies are actually more 'advanced' than they seem. Besides, it does not automatically follow that a miracle is false because the claimant comes from a time or place which Hume thinks isn't yet developed enough.
- The claims of 'competing' religions might raise questions about how far miracles claimed by different religions can all be true. But, again, it does not automatically follow that they cannot be true. Perhaps different religions experience different miracles, or interpret miraculous events differently.

Most religious people would probably argue against Hume's views. For them, their divine being/beings have the power and ability to change the laws of physics as they see fit. (In religions without divine beings, there may be powers and experiences which are beyond our explanation.) However, from a scientific and a philosophical perspective, such claims require evidence and also require to be reasonable. For many, the evidence is lacking, inconclusive, or contradictory, and, equally, the arguments are not reasonable – and so they argue that claims of miracles should be rejected.

Personal Reflection

- ✳ *Do you think miracles can be explained scientifically?*
- ✳ *What might be the benefits and drawbacks of using physical/psychological explanations to account for all miracles?*
- ✳ *What would count as proof that a miracle had happened?*

Apply your learning

Active Learning

1. Choose one miracle you have studied. As a group, consider how science might explain this miracle. Present your findings as a report.
2. Find examples of optical illusions and other examples of how our senses are sometimes fooled. Create a display of your findings.
3. Based on what you have learned in this chapter, how easy (or difficult) do you think it would be to convince people that you had experienced a miracle? As a group, discuss the factors involved for people to accept something as a miracle.
4. Some argue that religious worship and events are designed to create the conditions where people experience extraordinary things. Explore the worship/practices of one or more religions. How might these religions engage in practices which could lead to extraordinary experiences? Present your findings in an appropriate format.

Investigate

Find out more about:

➤ 'cold reading' and other claims/counter-claims about psychic powers
➤ the Barnum effect
➤ scientific views about 'consciousness' and 'altered consciousness'
➤ visual/aural and other sensory hallucinations
➤ inattention blindness
➤ the reliability of memory and eyewitness testimony
➤ the life of David Hume.

For each of these, report your findings in a manner of your choice. This could be a written report or presentation – in the form of tables, graphs and charts – or as the source of material for a class debate or discussion. You should select a method for your report which is most appropriate for the aspect you are investigating.

Check Your Understanding

1 What techniques are used in the opener for this chapter to suggest that mind reading is taking place?
2 In what ways might humans be 'meaning-seeking' and how might this affect our response to miracles?
3 What is meant by 'patternicity' and how might this link to miracles?
4 Why might a religious person believe in miracles?
5 What is 'science'?
6 Describe two possible scientific explanations for miracles based on physical factors.
7 How might a religious person respond to one of the physical explanations you described in the previous question?
8 What does 'biopsychosocial' mean and what is the connection with miracles?
9 Describe two possible psychological explanations for miracles.
10 How might a religious person respond to one of the psychological explanations you described in the previous question?
11 What claims about miracles were made by David Hume?
12 How might a religious person respond to Hume's position about miracles?

Analyse and Evaluate

1 'Miracles break the laws of physics, so they cannot happen.' Discuss this claim.
2 Analyse the view that miracles have perfectly rational explanations and so are not evidence for a divine being/beings.
3 To what extent might a religious person accept explanations for miracles offered by science?
4 'Miracles are unreasonable, therefore they are false.' Discuss.
5 Analyse the view that the unreliability of human memory makes miracle claims unlikely to be true.

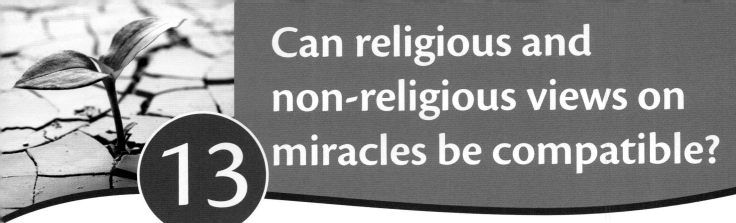

13 Can religious and non-religious views on miracles be compatible?

We are in the home of Andronicus, a powerful, but quite unpleasant, high-ranking Roman military commander in first-century Judaea. His reputation for the cruel treatment of his servants and his soldiers is well known. Andronicus has a 12-year-old daughter, Aurelia, who is agreed by all to be a delightful child and very different from her nasty father. Strangely, Andronicus is nothing but pleasant to his daughter, protecting her fiercely and even demonstrating the possibility of a softer side to his nature, which rarely has an outing in any other circumstance. However, all is not well. In fact, Aurelia is not well – very ill indeed, perhaps dying. Andronicus has had the best physicians attend to her, and one or two who have failed to improve her situation have disappeared in mysterious circumstances. Andronicus has heard that the daughter of a local Jewish man, Jairus, has been cured from serious illness – some say raised from the dead. Andronicus has a heated conversation with one of his very worried physicians, whose concern is not just for Aurelia …

Andronicus: A travelling Jewish teacher can raise someone from the dead, and yet you cannot even reduce Aurelia's fever!

Physician: Master, I have tried all that is known to physicians across all the empire.

Andronicus: Then try harder! Take from any empire, anywhere! Do your job, or it will be your last job, and your last breath!

Physician: We have all tried, master. We have worked tirelessly night and day and we all wish for Aurelia's health to improve. Everything — we have tried everything.   →

13 CAN RELIGIOUS AND NON-RELIGIOUS VIEWS ON MIRACLES BE COMPATIBLE?

137

Andronicus: And yet nothing has worked. But not so far away, the son of a builder raises a girl from the dead with but two words.

Physician: Master, we must treat such claims with caution. The people are ignorant; they are superstitious — they will believe whatever they want to believe. They hear a story, and they jump to conclusions about the power of their God. Not even the Emperor can raise from the dead. They are deluded.

Andronicus: So it is all a lie. She was not healed; she was not raised from the dead?

Physician: Who can say what the truth is? Some say she was simply asleep and the teacher awoke her.

Andronicus: Are you telling me that these people are so stupid that they cannot tell the difference between a sleeping daughter and a lifeless one?

Physician: Some claim so. As I said, they are an ignorant people — ready to believe anything.

Andronicus: And yet they believe. They have hope. Hope — where I have none. None, though you claim to have all the medical knowledge of the greatest empire the world has ever known!

Physician: We are doing all that we can, master.

Andronicus: THEN DO MORE! If it does not end well for Aurelia, then it will not end well for you. In fact, this Jewish teacher — have him brought here. Perhaps he can save my Aurelia — and if he does not, then you and he will face death together. Two healers who could not heal.

Physician: Master, do you really want these people to think that the might of Rome is in need of some ragged holy man?

Andronicus: The might of Rome cannot so far save my Aurelia. BRING HIM HERE ... NOW!

The healing of Jairus' daughter

The Bible tells the story of Jesus' healing of the daughter of Jairus. Jairus was a Jewish man who had heard the power of Jesus claimed by his followers. He rushed out to meet Jesus and asked that he return with him to heal his sick daughter – because he believed that Jesus had this power. Jesus agreed but, in one account of the story, the daughter was already dead by the time he arrived at the house. Jesus is said to have told Jairus that his daughter was not dead but asleep. He went to her bedside, uttered the Aramaic 'Talitha koum' and the girl arose, healed.

This is a typical example of a miracle – an alteration to the normal laws of physics. The question this section will consider is how far religious and non-religious views about miracles can be compatible. There are likely to be three possible responses:

1   Religious and non-religious views on miracles are completely *compatible*.
2   Religious and non-religious views on miracles are completely *incompatible*.
3   Religious and non-religious views on miracles are *in some ways* compatible.

For some Christians, the story of Jairus' daughter is to be understood literally – as something that happened exactly as described – a miraculous event carried out by Jesus. This would mean breaking the laws of physics and so would be incompatible with a non-religious view which understood the laws of physics to be unchangeable. Other Christians might take this to be a story which is not literally true, but which represents a truth – the power of Jesus and the belief that he was the son of God/God incarnate. This means that Jesus would not have literally raised Jairus' daughter from the dead but that he did something which might have seemed that way to onlookers. There would be no need to break any laws of physics so this would be compatible with a non-religious view that such a miracle can't occur. Many Christians take the view that believing such stories are literally true is what their faith is all about, while others can accept such stories as metaphors while still retaining their belief.

Let's now consider the three possible responses about compatibility between religious and non-religious views about miracles.

Religious and non-religious views about miracles are completely incompatible

- **Literal truth** When you take something literally you believe it to be absolutely true, without any doubt in your mind. You believe it as a matter of faith. For many religious people, accepting the literal truth of their scriptures and the claims of their religion is very important to them. They believe that you cannot pick and choose what you believe and what you don't believe. There is a danger that to start rejecting some aspects of your faith might lead to you rejecting it in its entirety. In their view, the best approach is to accept it all unquestioningly. This does not mean that you send your brain out to lunch, nor that you might somehow be deluding yourself – it's about accepting things as they are stated and living your life accordingly. You still think, but at the same time you accept the positions of your faith as completely true. For some theists, this approach is based on the idea that your God/the gods are beings of absolute power. Therefore they can do anything, and you must accept that as reality. You may not understand why certain things happen, but that is the nature of belief. You don't need to understand (not all of the time, at any rate) – you just believe. So if a story claims that God sent a range of plagues, then you accept that this is what he did. For other religious groups, miracles may be more about the power of the mind but still accepted as literally true. If Buddhist teaching states that the Buddha could leave his body and travel to other places, then that's exactly what he did – because that's exactly what a mind in this state makes it possible to do. It would be very difficult for a non-religious person to accept claims like these because doing so would mean agreeing that the laws of physics can be altered and amended at the whim of God/gods/special people.

- **Scriptural miracles** For many religious people, scriptures are the direct word of God/the gods/the teachings of the faith. Therefore they should be accepted as literally true in all respects. You cannot accept some as literal truth and some as metaphor. To do this would confuse your understanding of the faith and make it difficult to decide what is and isn't true. Therefore it is better to accept it all as true. Some also believe that scriptures are inspired/communicated by their divine being(s). Why would they communicate something which wasn't true? It is therefore necessary to accept scriptures as literal truths. This would be incompatible with a non-religious view which believed that altering the laws of physics is not possible, no matter what religious scriptures claim.

- **Miracles over nature** For many religious people, it is literally the case that Jesus walked on water, the Buddha transformed his body, the seas were parted to let the Israelites through, and so on. In their view, these actions are possible because divine beings (and beings of great power) are exactly what their faith claims them to be. For example, in Judaism and Christianity, God is believed to have created the universe and all the laws which apply to it. He is therefore able to alter these laws at any time, in any way, and for whatever purpose he chooses. He might do this as a demonstration of his power, or as a practical means to an end. Some non-religious people might challenge such beliefs because they go against the laws of nature. Even if God/the gods made these laws, it would not be appropriate for him/them to suddenly ignore them. This would make a mockery of their creation in the

13 CAN RELIGIOUS AND NON-RELIGIOUS VIEWS ON MIRACLES BE COMPATIBLE?

139

first place and it would raise the tricky question of why do it sometimes and not at other times? If nature miracles really happened in scriptural times, why not nowadays? Some argue that they do, while others say the evidence is a lot less obvious than it was in scriptural times. Obviously believing in these miracles as literally true would not be compatible with a non-religious view which understood the laws of physics to be unchangeable. These, in fact, might prove particularly troublesome miracles to accept since the sheer scale and power of such miracles would demand something really quite special of the person/being causing them.

> **Miraculous food** These miracles demonstrate an element of the power of God/the gods over natural forces and so are ways of showing divine power. Some say that they demonstrate divine concern for humans in need and are small, simple acts which tell us something about the nature of the divine. Non-religious people might ask why these miracles were so prevalent in scriptural times but aren't today. If God could send down 'manna from heaven', feed five thousand and turn water into wine – why not respond to human starvation in the same way today? Again, non-religious people are likely to argue that you cannot create something from nothing, and you cannot change one

substance into another (such as water into wine – not without the process of fermentation first!), therefore believing in the literal truth of such miracles would be incompatible with a non-religious view.

> **Healing miracles** These show power over nature and for many religious people are clear evidence of divine ability. They also show God's/the gods' concern for human suffering but, again, non-religious people might argue that if God/the gods could heal people of incurable disease, and even return them from the dead, in scriptural times, why not now? There are also some issues here about the use of people in this way and the fairness of it all. If accounts of healings are true, then why not heal everyone who was afflicted at the time, instead of just a chosen few? And why not raise all the dead, instead of just two people? Furthermore, why afflict people with illness and disease in the first place? Why do religious people rejoice in the miraculous healing of a few people and not question the absence of healing of the vast majority? Again, accepting these as literal events would be incompatible with a non-religious view which would argue that you can't change the laws of physics.

> **Power over demons** This is clearly based upon the belief in the existence of demons, demonic possession and all things of that nature. For many religious people today, such beings exist and can explain some afflictions. Therefore the reality of deliverance from demonic possession and its effects is literally true. Of course, non-religious people are unlikely to accept the truth of demons and other spiritual horrors. They would question the basic truth of deliverance from demonic possession, and discount such 'miracles'. The possible existence of demons (and so their casting out) raises a lot of questions about the laws of physics. Are such beings physical? If so, where do they live? What do they eat? It may be that religious people consider such beings to be spiritual beings rather than physical ones, and so they are not subject to the laws of physics. (However, some religious people will think of them as physical and so perhaps they are subject to the laws of physics.) Believing in demons in the first place is probably something which is incompatible with having a non-religious view of life, and believing that they cause illness and disease and can be 'cast out' is probably also likely to be incompatible with non-religious belief.

> **Modern-day miracles** No matter what category the miracle falls into, those who accept them as literally true will argue that they show the power of God/the gods over a range of forces; they are means of communicating truths to humans, no matter what form they take; they may demonstrate divine concern for human welfare; and they must be accepted as true otherwise humans would start to make their own decisions about which of their beliefs to accept and which to reject – and there are risks associated with this. Non-religious people would question what they see as

unquestioning acceptance, arguing that beliefs, too, should be approached critically and using our intelligence. They might especially question some modern 'miracles' such as weeping statues and, of course, would offer what they see as far more rational explanations for these events, which we will go on to explore.

So, in fact, whether the miracle is reported in a religion's scriptures or by those who witness or experience it in today's world probably makes no difference to the compatibility of religious and non-religious views about miracles. As long as a miracle is understood as a violation of the laws of physics, it is unlikely to be accepted by a non-religious person.

Talk Point

Should religious people accept miracles as literally true?

Religious and non-religious views about miracles are completely compatible

This position is most likely to be reached only where miracles are not accepted as literally true. If a religious or non-religious person could understand a miracle as something that only *appears* to break the laws of physics but does not actually do so, then perhaps they could accept them as 'true'. (Remember that many religious people do accept that miracles break the laws of physics.) In this way, both a religious and non-religious person could perhaps accept the events as something out of the ordinary but not actually 'miraculous'. So, for example, they might be prepared to accept that those who saw/reported/experienced 'miracles' believe them to be so, but they themselves would not actually accept that they are because no laws of physics were broken! This means that religious and non-religious people would only really be compatible in their beliefs if they understood miracles differently. A non-religious person would not conclude that they had been carried out by any divine beings since they wouldn't accept the existence of divine beings in the first place. However, they could accept that they were not able to be explained using current scientific methods or principles, on the understanding that such an explanation would likely be available at some point in the future.

Religious and non-religious views about miracles are in some ways compatible

This position is possible where it is agreed that miracles can be interpreted metaphorically, not literally. Something is metaphorical when it is representative of other things. It may be symbolic – in that one thing stands for another – or it may be a use of language where what is described is not meant to be taken as literally true but as a signpost to something which is true. It may also be a way of communicating something which is otherwise difficult to express. Metaphorical language might use simile (saying that something is 'like' something else), which might be especially useful when trying to explain something which is actually unlike anything that we know! Metaphorical language might use allegory – where language is used to symbolise or represent some deeper meaning which is otherwise difficult to convey. Religious people often interpret miracles metaphorically. They consider them not to be literally true, but pointers to something else or representative of some deeper meaning. For some, this enables them to cope with some of the more odd miracles, as well as account for the possibility of divine beings breaking their own laws or the laws of physics being broken. For some, this also helps them to deal with the possibility that miracles described in scripture no longer take place today, which takes care of the 'not now, but then' issue. The difficulty with this is that accepting miracles as metaphors might mean that you should accept all aspects of your faith as potential metaphors – including God/the gods. If you don't accept miracles as literally true, why should you accept it of any other aspect of your religion?

▶ **Scriptural miracles** For many religious people, their scriptures are regarded as complex mixtures of genres of writing which have been passed down through the ages. In the transmission of these scriptures, text has been altered.

13 CAN RELIGIOUS AND NON-RELIGIOUS VIEWS ON MIRACLES BE COMPATIBLE?

141

Sometimes this was done on purpose – to stress one thing over another – and at other times it might have been the result of copying errors or faltering memory, and so on. Even where stories have been passed down completely accurately, scriptures have to be understood in relation to the time and context in which they were written. People in the past may have understood the world differently and we must take this into account when reading scriptures with modern eyes. In relation to miracles, we have to consider why people understood things as they did, even though we might explain these things very differently today. How we understand the world around us has changed greatly over time, so religious people might argue that we have to interpret scriptural miracles differently today compared to the people who first heard them. This is not to say that scriptural miracles are untrue – it is just that they are considered to be true in a variety of ways, but not necessarily literally. In this way, religious and non-religious views could be compatible, since both could accept that the scriptural accounts of miracles are a product of their time and place and should not therefore be taken literally.

▶ **Miracles over nature** It is possible that such miracles have some truth in them, but not the whole truth. Perhaps the miracles over nature were in the mind of those who witnessed them, rather than real physical events – and there could be many reasons why such events were more 'in the mind' than in reality. Perhaps the stories became exaggerated and expanded in their transmission, so that subsequent accounts claimed more than the original – and more than really happened. Perhaps there is a link to truth without it being cause and effect truth. Perhaps the Egyptians did drown in their pursuit of the Israelites, but it was due to something other than a mighty closure of the seas. They may have halted at the sea for some reason and in later accounts this was conveyed as the sea closing. Non-religious people might find a lot to contest in relation to miracles over nature. If they were just stories, why the need for such fantastical events – which only really raise questions about their truth? If they were exaggerations, why the need for this? Perhaps unexaggerated but believable stories are of more value than wildly exaggerated and unlikely ones. Again, religious and non-religious views could be compatible here since no one is trying to hold on to the position that such miracles over nature actually happened as described and therefore broke the laws of physics.

▶ **Miraculous food** Some argue that the miraculous creation of foods is not a physical alteration of the laws of physics but an equally miraculous behavioural shift. For example, the story of the feeding of the five thousand claims that Jesus miraculously turned a few fish and some bread into enough food for such high numbers. Those who interpret this metaphorically might argue that what actually happened was a miracle of human behaviour – the boy who offered the loaves and fish to Jesus set an example to others, both in his faith in Jesus' ability to feed five thousand with the small offering and in his generosity in giving up his lunch. This motivated everyone else to produce their own, previously hidden, food stores, and all this was shared around equally. The miracle is in the change of heart of the crowd, not a physical alteration of food. Non-religious people are likely to argue that such interpretations are clutching at straws – turning what is reported as miraculous into something a lot less so, while still hanging on to some idea of the miraculous. However, if the religious person is not claiming the event as an alteration of the laws of nature to produce food out of nothing, or turn one thing into another, then perhaps an element of compatibility of viewpoints is possible.

▶ **Healing miracles** Understanding these as metaphor means perhaps altering your understanding of illness. Some argue that divine beings might use their knowledge to transform people and that this might be interpreted as deliverance from illness. Perhaps Jairus' daughter was not dead, or perhaps the story did not happen – it was simply a story to support belief in the power of Jesus. Some point out that how people understood and treated illness in the past was different from today, and so while the events described did happen, they did not happen as physical realities but as stories designed to communicate a message. Perhaps, too, the deliverance from physical illness was more a deliverance from its effects on people's thinking. Perhaps the person was not healed of the illness, but the personal and social consequences of the illness were healed. Again, removing the supernatural element of the event might make it possible for religious and non-religious views to be compatible to an extent.

▶ **Power over demons** Non-religious and many religious people reject belief in demons and demonic possession. Some might argue that the healing involved in these miracles was a physical healing, but not the casting out of an evil spirit. This links to the fact that people in the past would have understood such illnesses to be caused by demons, and so removal of the demon would end the illness. We can understand why people thought this, but at the same time disagree that this was literally the case. If a religious person is prepared to reject the existence of real demonic beings and explain the 'miracle' as something more figurative, then there could be an element of compatibility with the views of a non-religious person.

- **Modern-day miracles** No matter what the claim, or the evidence for or against, many religious people will take the view that modern miracles should be understood metaphorically. God/the gods are unlikely to visit miracles upon some and not others. And God/the gods are unlikely to randomly alter the laws of physics which he/they are responsible for. Such a universe would be an unpredictable and pretty random place, and so the literal truth of miracles should be called into question. Religious people might add that some modern miracles (and many of those from the past) have perfectly acceptable alternative explanations. Taking this view would allow some compatibility with non-religious views about miracles.

It is important to be aware that many religious people will also accept alternative explanations for miracles, while still accepting the beliefs and values of their faith and continuing to engage in its practices and traditions. Many religious people will accept philosophical and scientific explanations for miracles but also still hold their religious beliefs. Perhaps this 'compartmentalisation' is another way for religious and non-religious views to be, to an extent, compatible.

Summary

It is likely that it would be difficult for religious and non-religious people to reach any kind of agreement about the truth of miracles. They could agree that people have experienced strange and unusual events but they're not likely to agree about what these mean – and certainly not that they provide support for belief in a God. Both are approaching miracles from very different views of the world and this is unlikely to lead to their views being fully compatible. Perhaps the only possibility here is the same as for many topics in this book: agreeing to disagree. The solution might be for religious and non-religious people simply to accept that there are a great many things on which they might never agree – and just get on with making the world a better place, regardless of their differences of opinion.

Personal Reflection

- *Can religious and non-religious perspectives ever agree on the truth of miracles and does this matter?*
- *What (if any) evidence would you require before you accepted a miracle as literally true?*
- *Some argue that accepting miracles as metaphors demands more faith than accepting them as literally true. What do you think?*

13 CAN RELIGIOUS AND NON-RELIGIOUS VIEWS ON MIRACLES BE COMPATIBLE?

143

Apply your learning

Active Learning

1 Write an article for a religious magazine discussing the story of Jairus' daughter and the implications of it for religious belief. Ensure that your article explores the story from both a literal and a metaphorical position.

2 Choose a report of a miracle from a religion other than the Judaeo-Christian tradition and carry out the same activity as in **1** above. Alternatively, produce a range of investigative questions you would ask about this claimed miracle.

3 Carry out your own research into people's views about some of the miracles covered in this chapter. Devise your own questionnaire or short interview to find out their views about these miracles. Ask questions which will help you to show how religious people approach miracles differently and the difference between religious and non-religious responses to claims about miracles. Report your findings anonymously.

4 Choose a few of the miracles you have considered, or those from other faiths and contexts, and produce a series of 'alternative explanations' for these miracles.

Investigate

Find out more about:

➤ other scriptural miracles across a range of faiths, including the variety of interpretations of these miracles within and across faiths

➤ how scriptures were transmitted down through the ages and what issues this might raise

➤ modern claims of miracles – who made the claim, where did the miracle take place and what do they say happened? Investigate possible responses to these miracle claims.

For each of these, report your findings in a manner of your choice. This could be a written report or presentation – in the form of tables, graphs and charts – or as the source of material for a class debate or discussion. You should select a method for your report which is most appropriate for the aspect you are investigating.

Check Your Understanding

1   Describe the story of Jairus' daughter and the issues it might raise for religious people.
2   What does it mean to accept something as literally true?
3   Does accepting something as literally true mean you don't think about it?
4   In what different ways might someone accept something as metaphorically true?
5   Is accepting something metaphorically the same thing as rejecting it as literally true?
6   Describe two types of scriptural miracles and the issues presented by accepting them as literally true.
7   Are any special issues presented by accepting modern-day miracles as literally true?
8   Describe two scriptural miracles and how they might be explained as metaphors.
9   Some might argue that treating a scriptural miracle as metaphor shows a lack of faith. What responses might be given to this?
10 Does accepting modern miracles as metaphors present different issues from accepting scriptural miracles as metaphors?
11 Could a non-religious person accept that miracles happen?
12 Is it possible that some miracles are more believable than others? How might religious and non-religious people categorise miracles in this way?

Analyse and Evaluate

1   'Accepting the literal truth of miracles is the only position a religious person can ever justify.' Discuss this claim.
2   'Religious and non-religious people will never agree about miracles.' Discuss.
3   To what extent must a religious person accept scriptural miracles as literally true?
4   'Compatibility between religious and non-religious views on miracles is only possible where miracles are understood metaphorically.' How far do you agree with this claim?

Revision guidance and exam-type questions

Some SQA and other guidance

There have been changes to the SQA 'Religious and Philosophical Questions' unit since the first edition of this book was published. This second edition aims to reflect these changes but you should always check with your teacher that you are following the latest course guidance. This is especially true if you are using this book on your own to supplement what you are doing in class. The SQA can change course content, and it takes time for a new edition of any book to catch up with this. This is especially true also in relation to SQA exam question types. This book suggests *exam-type* questions. It does not contain any actual exam questions from past papers – or from any future papers! The questions are there to help you with your revision towards the actual exam.

Current course specifications, past paper questions, marking instructions and a whole load of other useful stuff for this course has very kindly been provided by the SQA. You can find all of this on the SQA website for Higher RMPS at https://www.sqa.org.uk/sqa/47911.html (though bear in mind that website addresses can change too!).

According to the SQA, through studying this unit of the Higher RMPS course, *'Candidates develop skills to critically analyse religious and philosophical questions and responses ... This course helps candidates to understand society. They learn about, and from, religious beliefs, non-religious viewpoints, and personal experience. By exploring how religion, morality and philosophy can help people find meaning and purpose in life, candidates develop their understanding of human beliefs, values and behaviour.'* It is hoped that you will build up a balanced and well-understood picture of religious and philosophical questions and how religious and non-religious groups respond to these. This will also – and very importantly – help you to further develop your own beliefs and values which Curriculum for Excellence Religious and Moral Education has been helping you to do since you were in Early Years. Now that you are in your senior phase of education, you should be building upon the prior learning you have been engaged in since you were very young. This doesn't stop at the end of your Higher RMPS course (or Advanced Higher if you go on to give that a go). It is a lifelong process. It is hoped that studying this course will develop very important skills for learning, life and work and support you throughout your life.

How to study

There is not just one way to revise – everyone learns in different ways, and different ways of revising work for different people. You have to find the method(s) which work best for you. Whatever its form, revision means *processing* the information, facts and figures, viewpoints, opinions and so on in this course. Processing means engaging in a range of skills which will help you to understand the materials you have covered in this course: processing is a circular and so never-ending process and is sometimes reduced to the term 'Plan, Do, Review'. In practice, one way of thinking about processing is this:

▶ **Gather your information** Use this book and as many other resources as you have time to. Pull together the information and make careful notes about where it comes from.

▸ **Organise your information** Put the information together under the following headings: facts, figures, opinions, beliefs, arguments, counter-arguments; then sort it into categories of 'for' and 'against', 'religious' and 'non-religious', and whatever other categories make sense to you.

▸ **Review your information** What is everything you have gathered telling you? How do you know if what you have gathered is true, authentic, valid, reliable and representative? How up to date is your information? Where did it come from? Who said it? What might that person (or group) have to gain by saying this?

▸ **Assess your information** How does what you have gathered increase your understanding? What questions remain and how will you answer these?

▸ **Redraft your information** Processing of information is often helped by redrafting the information you have gathered. This forms new neural connections in your brain and so helps you to understand the material better (and probably remember it better too). So, can you turn your information into a picture, a diagram, a song, a speech, a doodle, a word cloud, a 'thing', a painting, a sculpture, a dance …? The more you can do with your information, the more neural connections you're making and so the more effectively you will learn it.

▸ **Use your information** Devise a range of questions about your issue/topic and use your information to answer these. Think creatively – you could come up with some very serious questions (Why does X agree with evolution?) or some less serious ones (Would a plumber be less likely to believe in a miracle than a teacher?) to help you get a different perspective on an issue.

It's worth pointing out that a lot of thinking at the moment says that we are far more likely to learn effectively when we do it in collaboration with others. This might not be true for everyone, of course, but learning with others can be helpful and enjoyable – so working together with others can help you to develop your understanding even further as you debate, argue, discuss and support each other in your learning.

You can buy lots of books on revision skills and techniques and there are many websites which help with revision too. You can also get hold of past papers in RMPS from the SQA website as well as a range of other guidance about RMPS.

Exam-type questions

You can find sample exam papers and the marking instructions on the SQA website, and subsequent papers and marking instructions will be there too. **The questions which follow are not official SQA exam questions, but are similar to the types of questions you can expect in your SQA exam.**

Questions in the Religious and Philosophical Questions component of the exam paper will be worth 20 marks each.

Presenting well-structured and reasoned views

The Religious and Philosophical Questions section of the RMPS exam is in Paper 2. For this part of the exam, the SQA states that '*This question paper assesses the skills of applying in-depth knowledge and understanding, analysing and evaluating religious, moral and philosophical questions and presenting reasoned and well-structured views.*'

It is important to remember that all the question stems which follow are for example only, and so you should keep up to date with the kinds of question stems which are used in future RMPS exams.

Also, the SQA can only ask questions in the examination which link to the mandatory content of the course as set out in the Course Specification. The questions below are not real SQA exam questions, they are 'exam-type questions'. The longer this course runs, the more past exam papers will be available for you to be able to work out the kinds of question which are likely to be asked.

Here are some examples:

1 'Everything was created.' Discuss this claim.
2 Discuss the view that the origin of the universe requires a creator.
3 To what extent can a religious person accept scientific explanations for the origins of life?
4 How far can religious and non-religious people agree about the origins of the universe?

5   To what extent can a religious person accept scientific explanations for the Big Bang?
6   'Scientific accounts of the origins of life show that there is no need for a creator.' Discuss this claim.
7   'Belief in God can be rejected using argument alone.' Discuss.
8   How far religious people successfully defend belief in the existence of a God?
9   To what extent must a religious person accept the teleological argument?
10   'Belief in God is about belief, not argument.' Discuss.
11   How far can the existence of God be proved?
12   'Humans are responsible for suffering and evil.' Discuss.
13   To what extent are suffering and evil the responsibility of God?
14   How far is it reasonable to accept the literal truth of miracles?
15   To what extent must religious people accept miracles in scripture?
16   'Scriptural miracles are no longer relevant in today's world.' Discuss.
17   To what extent can a religious person reject miracles and still hold religious belief?
18   'When someone says they have experienced a miracle, they are simply deluding themselves.' Discuss this claim.

Constructing your exam answer

The SQA provides clear marking instructions for those who will mark your exam paper. The marking instructions are in two groups, General Marking Instructions and Specific Marking Instructions.

General marking instructions

These give very broad principles which markers will apply when assessing your answer. You are required to show knowledge and understanding, analysis and evaluation skills.

1   **Knowledge and understanding**
     This could include providing information which is accurate and relevant; providing references to sources, case studies and/or examples and viewpoints; describing arguments.
2   **Analysis**
     This could include making links between different things and the whole, including related concepts; similarities and things which are contradictory; things which are consistent and inconsistent; different views and interpretations; consequences and implications; showing that you understand order and structure and that you can demonstrate the relative importance of components.
3   **Evaluation**
     This could include how relevant, important or useful a view or source is; positive and negative features of a view or source; strengths and weaknesses of a view or source; other evaluative comments.

Specific marking instructions

These specific instructions guide markers towards knowing what should be present in an answer and therefore what an excellent/good/awful answer looks like. In a 20 mark question, a maximum of 10 marks are available for KU which is relevant to the question and detailed, up to 5 marks are available for analytical comments and up to 5 marks are available for reasoned evaluative comments.

To help you with this, we'll use a typical exam-type question.

▶   **Question** 'How far is belief in miracles possible for both religious and non-religious people?'
▶   **Purpose** This question is designed to give you the opportunity to explore and reach a conclusion about how far religious and non-religious people can agree about miracles. Remember that your answer to this question can be based on any religion/scriptures and can take any view about the question which you are able to justify.

Specific instructions

Knowledge and Understanding (up to 10 marks available) may include:

▶ Description of one or more types of miracle.
▶ Discussion of the possible questions and issues this miracle raises for religious people and/or non-religious people.
▶ Using sources which support religious/non-religious viewpoints.

Analysis (up to 5 marks available) may include:

▶ Analysing religious and non-religious viewpoints about miracles.
▶ Analysing sources.

Evaluation (up to 5 marks available) may include:

▶ Providing a judgement about the strengths/weaknesses of religious/non-religious views on miracles.
▶ Providing a judgment about how far religious and non-religious people can agree about miracles (i.e. how far their views are compatible).

A final word

Hopefully your RMPS course will mean more to you than an 'A' pass – though that would be nice too. Hopefully it will help you to understand yourself and others better and so get more out of life and give more in life. The whole point of learning is to make the world a better place. It is sometimes too easy to think that there is nothing we can do to make the world better, but if we all do a little, then that will amount to a great deal. I wish you well in your study of this subject and course, and that you keep learning throughout your life.

Index